How *to* Honor
Your Aging
Parents

How to Honor Your Aging Parents

Fundamental Principles of Caregiving

Richard P. Johnson, Ph.D.

ONE LIGUORI DRIVE, LIGUORI, MO, 63057-9999

Imprimi Potest:
Richard Thibodeau, C.Ss.R.
Provincial, Denver Province
The Redemptorists

ISBN 0-7648-0476-6
Library of Congress Catalog Card Number: 99-71466

Scripture quotations are from the *New Revised Standard Version of the Bible*, copyright © 1989 by the Division of Christian Education of the National Council of the Churches of Christ in the USA. Used with permission. All rights reserved.

This book is a thoroughly revised edition of *Aging Parents—How to Understand and Help Them*, © 1987, Liguori Publications.

To order, call 1-800-325-9521
http://www.liguori.org

Cover design by Ross M. Sherman
Cover Image Tony Stone

TABLE OF CONTENTS

INTRODUCTION

I wrote this book because I have seen too many wonderful people, from all faiths and walks of life, confront the role of caregiving and fail. They were unprepared for the caregiving role, and so they became exhausted and exasperated, muddled and mired in guilt. Eventually, they lost something of themselves. Many of these well-meaning adult children quietly persevered, but they felt the sting of self-reproach and the emptiness of despondency all too often. These were not bad, lazy, or negligent people; they were good folks, energetic and kind. They wanted the very best for their aging parent, relative, or friend. Most of them simply tried to do too much—trying to control a situation which was clearly uncontrollable. It hurt me anew each time I saw another good caregiver emotionally "bite the dust," as it were.

This book is my attempt to prepare good people to do the best job possible, and truly honor their aging parent, relative, or friend without losing themselves in the process. I believe that caregiving can be the "master teacher" of life; I believe that the caregiving role can become a wellspring of strength and a door to grace unlike any other life endeavor.

Over the twenty or so years that I have worked with caregivers, I have come to realize that they fare best when they are equipped with solid information. I have compacted the essential information necessary for successful caregiving into *ten fundamental principles of caregiving*. In order to achieve the marvelous personal and spiritual heights that successful caregiving can offer, we must understand and use these fundamental caregiving principles. The degree to which we apply these will determine the degree of personal success in our caregiving journey.

These caregiving principles form the backbone of this book. When you apply them in your particular situation, they can spell the difference between merely surviving in your caregiving—at whatever level and type you may be called to do this—and dynamically thriving.

The book is written for any person who is—or anticipates that he or she will be—called upon to give some form of care to an elder. Sooner or later, most of us will enter the ranks of caregivers to older persons at some level. Most probably, this care will be required in support of your own parents, but care may also be required for other members of the immediate and extended family as well. Some may also be called upon to render direct care or supportive care to elder friends, neighbors, and to church and/or community members. The book is dedicated to all persons who render supportive care to elders in whatever form, at whatever level, and to whomever they render it.

My experience of working in this field convinces me that much can be done to enhance the basic caregiving role. These pages were written to share these convictions with you. It is hoped that this book will help you look at the elders for whom you care in a new, fresh way. Your primary caregiving goal is to achieve the best possible relationship. However, if success is to be realized in this important matter, you must not allow yourself to become overwhelmed in the process. This would help neither you nor your loved one.

The relationship between an adult child and an aging parent brings new challenges at every turn. We can successfully meet the challenges of caregiving if we have two things: First, we need a certain fund of knowledge about older persons, about caregiving, and about ourselves; second, we need to see the caregiving situation as an area of growth for ourselves—that we have something important to gain from the encounter. Our innate sense of good will simply isn't enough to carry us through.

When seen from a perspective of faith, caregiving becomes a triangle of love between God, you, and your aging parent (or other elder). When combining these principles with the faith-enhancing approach to caregiving that this book advocates, you are given the spiritual power needed to genuinely honor your aging parent as well as yourself.

While this book is focused primarily on the adult child/aging parent relationship, it is by no means restricted to this. Throughout the book I use the term "caregiver" to refer to anyone, an adult child or otherwise, who performs some service or renders some support to an elder. I like the term "elder" instead of "elderly." I believe the latter demeans older persons. Personally, I have no intention of becoming "an elderly," but I do have every intention of becoming "an elder." Elders, those receiving the care or service, may be an aging parent, a relative, friend, or even an acquaintance. All the principles discussed here can be applied to any caregiver/elder relationship.

By reading and using this book, you are taking a very positive step. You are helping yourself and, at the same time, helping your aging parent. It lifts my heart to see many eager adult children with one purpose in mind: to provide the best possible care to a loved one who is getting old. It is evident that what these devoted daughters and sons want most of all, despite all the difficulties, is to truly *honor* their aging father or mother, and that is a beautiful sight to see!

THE FIRST FUNDAMENTAL
PRINCIPLE OF CAREGIVING:

∽

You Cannot Honor Your Aging Parents by Dishonoring Yourself and/or Your Family

The Book of Exodus, chapter 20, verse 12, states the Fourth Commandment:

> *"Honor your father and your mother, so that your days may be long in the land that the LORD your God is giving you."*

The Fourth Commandment is perhaps the best known of the Ten Commandments in the Judeo-Christian tradition. Certainly, it is one of the first ones taught to children. And yet our understanding of it is frequently one-dimensional and quite elementary. That is not surprising. As youngsters, this commandment echoed through our minds as a central theme in our religious instruction. The basic message was that to honor meant "to obey." Period. If we obeyed our parents then we were honoring them. Of course, other aspects were mentioned, such as respect and love, but obedience was the main point. If we were obedient children, we knew we were "good"—we were keeping the commandment.

At that early level of religious formation this approach to

obedience made a lot of sense. We were instructed to demonstrate faith in our parents as the legitimate representatives of God for us in our lives here and now. To our small minds, our parents were indeed like giants, even godlike, and our religious training strengthened this perception over and over.

Your Parents

Viewing our parents in this light also fits in nicely with the emotional, mental, and social development of our personality. Indeed,

> *our faith in our parents provided the foundation of trust in ourselves*

—and those around us—necessary for healthy growth. Ultimately, our capacity for intimacy, that is, our ability to share our lives, innermost thoughts, feelings, and values—the cornerstone of emotional health—is a direct developmental consequence of our faith in our parents. Without this faith— developed very early in life—we would find it most difficult, if not impossible, to find peace in our lives. Without this faith, we would be overcome with suspiciousness, fraught with fear, and ever vigilant to protect our fragile egos from the attacks we thought were bombarding us.

- **Your parents were your first loves**

    Our first love relationships, those we had with our parents, created in us an emotional center which in large measure determined the degree to which we would be open to others. Whether we believe the world is a generally safe place where we can find comfort and satisfaction or a place of hostility that we must fight our way through, depends to a large extent on the trust we, as very young children, developed in our parents or significant others.

    Our father and mother taught us love; they were our "primary" love relationships in that they were "first." All other love relationships reflect to some degree the love relationship we formed with our parents. Faith and trust in our parents provided the crucial core of our emotional selves, a core which stands as the epicenter of our perceptions about ourselves and about the world in which we live. This core, of course, still lives and functions within us even though years have passed and we are now the adult children of aging and aged parents. Our parents, regardless of our age or theirs, are still our parents. We are still their children.

- **You will never be your aging parents' parent**

The Fourth Commandment echoes through our minds: "Honor your father and your mother." This will never change; we will always be children of our parents. We will never be their parents. Even though we are called at times to perform tasks which seem fundamentally parental for our own parents, the role reversal that has been so often touted as fact can never happen.

- **Update your thinking about the Fourth Commandment**

In practice, what does the Fourth Commandment mean now that we are adults? Should we continue to hold on to a limited understanding of this commandment, that is, should we focus principally on *obeying* the wishes of our parents just as we did when we were youngsters? If we are to change our definition of "to honor," where do we make the necessary modifications? How do we honor our parents' wishes if we feel these desires run counter to their well-being? Where is the boundary between their right to self-determination and our obligation to remain steadfast in our concern for them, and—when the time comes—to make prudent decisions regarding their health and welfare?

The Fourth Commandment bestows a responsibility on us based in love, to remain faithful to the ongoing welfare of our parents, but the Fourth Commandment never instructed us to give up ourselves in the process.

The Fourth Commandment

To get some help from the scriptural text itself, we turn to the scholarly *Interpreter's Bible* for clarification. There, perhaps to our surprise, we see that the original intent of the Fourth Commandment dealt precisely with our situation: the relationship between an adult child and an aging parent. The Fourth Commandment was primarily concerned with how adult children would provide care for a parent or other dependent who was experiencing the ravages of time and/or sickness. Only secondarily did this precept treat the taken-for-granted notion that young children should obey their parents.

The Fourth Commandment was principally a warning against the heathen practice of abandoning the aged when they could no longer support and care for themselves.

The ancient Israelites would have been acquainted with many examples of this barbarous custom. It was happening all the time in the surrounding societies. History tells us, however, that the practice wasn't limited to ancient peoples. Even into modern times, certain cultures have used this method of dealing with the aged or infirm, those who were unable to "keep up." Nor should we become smug ourselves, thinking we are beyond such uncivilized behavior: Is not the idea of active euthanasia—now lawful in some states and in some countries—at root derived from this "heathen habit"?

As children, "honor" meant obedience.
As adults, "honor" means remain steadfast.

Abandonment

The Book of Exodus does not mince words in describing what abandonment meant to the aged in those days, saying they are not to be sent abroad to be eaten by beasts or to die of exposure. Times have changed, but perhaps not all that much. Today's acts of abandonment may be more subtle, but they still fly in the face of the precept. A modern dictionary's definition of abandonment is only slightly broader: to withdraw protection, support, or help, or to exercise complete disinterest in the fate of.... Clearly, abandoning loved ones is an extreme form of dishonor. Like all violations of God's laws, it also dishonors those who do the abandoning. It separates the violators from the godliness which is supposed to be their biblical heritage, their part in the covenant, which is nothing but the sacred "contract" containing the obligations spelled out in the Ten Commandments.

The Fourth Commandment instructs us: "Do not abandon."

Abandonment is a rather imprecise word. What would be considered abandonment to one caregiver would only be quite natural for another. Each caregiving situation needs to be appraised individually to determine if any abandonment exists. What I find is that many caregivers over-define what would be considered abandonment. I dealt with a caregiver once who believed she had to visit her mother in the nursing home at least twice a day for two hours each time and that, if she didn't, it would be considered abandonment. I have dealt with other adult children who believe that a call around Christmas is enough contact. Obviously, to make the determination whether abandonment is present depends upon many variables, including the strength of the aging parent, resources, proximity of the caregiver, other assistance that the caregiver has at his or her disposal, and the like. Yet abandonment can be expressed on many levels and in many ways:

1. Physical abandonment: neglect of physical needs
2. Financial abandonment: failure to fund basic needs
3. Emotional abandonment: very little, if any, contact
4. Psychological abandonment: verbal abuse or neglect
5. Familial abandonment: cut off from family involvement
6. Spiritual abandonment: never talk about God or the hereafter

Saint Thomas Aquinas reminds us that when we "honor" our parents, we display a genuine piety toward them. We show a fidelity to our natural obligations and our duty to act in accord with the will of our loving God. Honor is intimately connected with justice, righteousness, and peace because it upholds the solidarity of the family. We show honor to our parents through a willingness to share our gifts with them. These gifts are not just our material possessions, but, even more so, respect, esteem, and reverence. At the same time, to honor our parents in this way certainly doesn't connote a blind obedience to each and every whim they might express.

- **Remember that honoring your aging parents does not mean abandoning yourself**

  Whereas the Fourth Commandment is clear about not abandoning your aging parent, it is not so clear about abandoning yourself. I see many caregivers who do exactly that: They give until they have but an ounce of energy left to give, which they then go ahead and give away as well. They are left with nothing of themselves; they are emotionally spent; their energies are all but exclusively devoted to their aging parent. While this may be necessary for short periods of time, as when your aging parent is in dire need, it is totally unnecessary and unhealthy for any such situation to persist over the long haul.

  There are many ways we can abandon ourselves:

1. Physical abandonment: neglect of one's own physical needs
2. Financial abandonment: failure to fund one's basic needs

3. Emotional abandonment: very little, if any, contact with friends
4. Psychological abandonment: verbal abuse or neglect toward oneself
5. Familial abandonment: cut off from own family involvement
6. Spiritual abandonment: forfeiture of one's faith and prayer

Norman's Story

Norman's eighty-five-year-old mother has lived with him since she fell and broke her hip three years ago. She had been quite helpful to Norman, himself a widower with grown children, doing the majority of the cooking and light housekeeping. Then, about three months ago, she began to act strangely. Norman found the gas range left on several times; her checkbook, which she formerly kept meticulously, ended up in a shamble; her personal hygiene deteriorated, along with her attention to just about any detail. Norman wants his mother to see a doctor about these changes; she adamantly refuses. How can Norman best honor his mother?

If Norman were to obey his mother's refusal, he would dishonor both himself and his mother. He would be overlooking her true needs; he would be pandering to her wants instead of dealing with her actual needs. This is not healthy for either party. Clearly, Norman doesn't want to take away one of his mother's fundamental human needs: that of making decisions for herself. Yet, if and when her decisions—or lack of decisions—render her increasingly vulnerable, it will become necessary for Norman to make the decisions, even when these decisions may be unpopular. Here is where "honoring" takes on a bit more difficult edge, where we need the most carefully considered judgment, and where we need to exercise adroit caution.

Sanctions

The Book of Exodus backs up the Fourth Commandment with two strong sanctions, one positive and one negative.

- **Caregiving characterized by honor brings unexpected riches**

Those who follow the commandment are given a promise: "...that your days may be long in the land" (21:12). To an agrarian society, land meant survival if not wealth. Those who were loyal to the directive could look forward to a long and "rich" life. If the whole society abided by the commandment, everyone, including the elders, could be confident of continued care without fear of abandonment.

This positive sanction still holds true today. You, too, will live a rich life as a consequence of honoring your aging parent. The gifts and benefits that accrue to you from successfully honoring your aging parent may not be as tangible as land, but they are the true source of all wealth. Riches such as patience, perseverance, stamina, hope, mercy, and charity all flow into caregivers who find ways to honor their aging parents more and more deeply.

- **Caregiving without honoring brings you loss**

The negative sanction is: "Whoever curses father or mother shall be put to death" (Exodus 21:17). Giving no honor to our parents is a form of curse. Dishonor doesn't bring physical death but an inner death to parts of ourselves. We experience the loss of honor, self-respect, and peace of mind. Dishonor brings death to our relationships, making them lifeless and shallow. Consequently, we miss out on a fundamental form of spiritual and psychological nourishment that gives life. When we dishonor, we deal "death-messages" to our own sense of self.

A version of this biblical death threat came to America with the Puritans. In *The Book of the General Laws of the Inhabitants of the Jurisdiction of New-Plimouth* (1685), it was stated: "If a child above the age of sixteen shall curse or smite his natural father or mother he shall be put to death." It is not known whether this threat was actually ever carried out. However, it is interesting to note that even the authoritarian Puritans recognized that mitigating circumstances could negate the extreme punishment of death. First, the death penalty would not be imposed if it could be proven that the parents had been "unchristianly negligent" in the education of their children. Evidently, children who had not been properly taught the Word of God were not held responsible for their "heathen" behavior. Secondly, no death penalty would be imposed upon children who had been so provoked by extreme and cruel correction by their parents that the children were forced to "curse or smite" their parents in self-defense, so as "to preserve themselves from death or maiming."

The relationship covered by the Fourth Commandment is a two-way street. In our present culture, it is unlikely that we will come across aged parents who are inflicting physical death or maiming on their adult children. However, it is not uncommon to discover parents who have so manipulated their adult children, or become so critical or demanding of them, that the adult children suffer near-fatal emotional or psychological wounds. This goes far beyond simply hurt feelings. Such manipulation can become so severe that the "psychological child" in the adult child dies or is seriously maimed.

As the Fourth Commandment admonishes adult children to honor their aging parents, so too, parents must honor their children. Moreover, all people involved must honor themselves. It is the only way the divine precept can be fully lived. The Fourth Commandment has the preservation of family solidarity as its central purpose. This cannot be fulfilled if an individual "makes light of" or "takes away from" his or her own person or family in deference to the demands of an aging parent. In other words, is it possible to honor part of God's creation by dishonoring another part?

Getting angry, holding resentments, feeling guilty, frustrated, overworked, or under-loved isn't the answer; expressing it calmly to someone who understands is the answer!

The Scale of Care for Aging Parents

This "Scale of Care for Aged Parents" is an effort to provide some guidelines for adult children so they can gauge the degree of honor (or dishonor) they give their aging parents and themselves. The scale is a 1-10 continuum which describes various styles of caring (or lack of caring).

DIRECTIONS: *Read each of the nine points on the scale. Rate each of the nine points on a scale from 1 to 10. A rating of 1 for any of the nine points indicates that this does not at all describe your behavior with your aging parent. A rating of 10, on the other hand, indicates that you believe that this statement describes your behavior with your aging parent to a very high degree. Ratings between 1 and 10 indicate varying degrees of accuracy in describing your behavior with your aging parent. Place your rating in the space provided to the left of each of the nine points on the continuum:*

Describes Me

1   2   3   4   5   6   7   8   9   10
not at all   to a high degree

_____ 1. *Violence and Active Abuse:* I inflict violence upon my aging parent in the form of physical, mental, or verbal abuse.

_____ 2. *Abandonment or Neglect:* I withhold protection or support from my aging parent, allowing life-threatening situations to persist.

_____ 3. *Indifference or Detachment:* I display poorly concealed indifference or deep irritation toward my aging parent; I maintain an air of detachment or aloofness toward my aging parent; I regard care of my aging parent only as an obligation.

____ 4. *General Support:* I quite freely give support to my aging parent. Even though I give this care with a guarded degree of warmth and respect, I nonetheless do show concern for his or her emotional, physical, and spiritual well-being.

____ 5. *Expressed Empathy and a Quality Relationship.* I exercise the ability to "be with" my aging parent on an emotional level. I strive to create a healthy relationship between myself and my aging parent where feelings can be freely expressed and received with nonjudgmental, mutual positive regard.

____ 6. *Sympathy:* A lot of the time I *do* experience feeling sorry for the aging parent. I find myself deeply regretting that he or she is suffering the losses that come with aging.

____ 7. *Occasional Overinvolvement:* The care I give to my aging parent is sometimes characterized by periodic attempts to "do for" rather than "be with."

____ 8. *Consistent Overinvolvement:* I frequently find myself thinking and worrying about my aging parent. I find myself being compulsively driven to do more for my aging parent. I know this is not good, but I can't seem to stop it.

____ 9. *Heroic Overinvolvement:* The care I give to my aging parent is frequently characterized by frantic and desperate attempts to provide for every possible need and want. I know this brings increased dependence upon me, but I don't know how to care for her/him any other way.

Scoring:
1. Add your ratings for items 1, 2 & 3 together: _____
2. Add your ratings for items 4, 5 & 6 together: _____
3. Add your ratings for items 7, 8 & 9 together: _____

Interpretation:
1. Score One is your "Dishonoring Aging Parents" score
2. Score Two is your "Caregiving Balance" score
3. Score Three is your "Dishonoring Self" score

Which of your three scores is the highest? Which is the lowest? Your highest score is where you focus the majority of your caregiving energy. Your lowest score is where you are investing the least amount. The ideal is to have the second score, "Caregiving Balance," as your highest score. It is here you find the best balance between "under-care" and "over-care." Neither of the two extremes is healthy: Score One indicates a position wherein you are not honoring your father and mother; Score Three indicates a position wherein you are not honoring yourself.

Personal Sharing Questions

1. Describe a situation where you wanted to honor a request of your aging parent while at the same time knowing that this would not be in his/her best interest.
2. Did you ever find yourself in a situation that seemed as if honoring your aging parent would mean dishonoring yourself and/or your family? Describe what you did.
3. Describe a situation when you wished to, or thought it best to say "no" to your aging parent, and yet you "gave in."
4. Where do you place yourself on the "Scale of Care"? Describe why you rate yourself there.

THE SECOND FUNDAMENTAL
PRINCIPLE OF CAREGIVING:

◦◦◦

*Understand the Real Needs of Your Aging
Parents and Distinguish These from the
"Wants" Your Parents May Request*

A second fundamental principle of caregiving is to understand the real needs of your aging parent, and to clearly separate those needs from all other desires or wants he or she may request. Once you understand what the needs are, you can move ahead with increased confidence. Unless and until you can separate needs from simple wants, you risk falling into a trap of fostering an increasing dependence in your aging parent. Dependence is often the primary personality distortion befalling older persons. It brings with it psychological damage to your parent while emotionally overburdening you.

- **Try to stay out of the middle**

We have all heard about the "generation gap." It usually refers to those differences in values, attitudes, and world-view between parents and their teenage children. There is another generation gap. It is the gap that exists between middle-aged parents of teens and their own parents. This generation gap places these middle-aged adult children squarely between their own teen/early adult children on the one hand and their aging parents on the other. These middle-aged parents are in a tenuous position. They are trying to be good parents for their own children, while at the same time trying to deal with the growing needs of their parents.

The Sandwich Generation

Two forces have converged to put middle-aged persons in such a generational squeeze. These middle-aged adults are sometimes called the "sandwich generation": they are caught between two generational phenomena occurring in our culture at the same time. It is as if they become like a piece of ham pressed between two slices of bread.

On the one hand, their own children are staying at home longer. Since 1950, the average marriage age has increased by more than four years. Add to that the so-called "revolving door" syndrome, the fact that a significant number of children elect to come home again after vacating their family of origin home for college or other work experience. The fact is that children are remaining dependents, in one form or another, much longer than in previous generations. The result is that their parents, now middle-aged, are carrying a longer, if not heavier, responsibility for dependent care.

On the other hand, their own aging parents are living much longer. Longevity figures continue to climb. Aging parents require care, or considered attention, to a greater degree than in previous generations. With every new medical procedure—every new rehabilitation regime put into place, every new miracle drug introduced, and every new surgical technique developed—the length of time we are spending here on earth is increasing.

It is the "sandwich generation" to whom both the younger and the older generations turn for support. At times, the burden of care from both sides can become overwhelming. A closer look at what is occurring in the lives of these sometimes beleaguered middle-aged caregivers, as contrasted with what is happening in the lives of their elder parents, might serve us well.

- **Continue investing in your career**

Let us start by asking about something that, by any reckoning, has taken up a considerable part of our life: our work, occupation, or career. How do middle-aged people regard their work? At once, we find some interesting differences between men and women.

Middle-aged males are in what is called the maintenance stage of their careers. They have expended lots of energy climbing the proverbial ladder, and the drive for career advancement has perhaps ebbed just a bit. Lifestyle concerns, rather than work accomplishment, take a more focused place in their lives. They are naturally still interested in advancement; however, they have realized that their promotions will certainly not come with the same frequency as in the past. This is not necessarily a negative awareness, but it does affect how they view themselves. Enter the aging parent!

For the middle-aged female, however, a somewhat different picture presents itself. She may well have been a homemaker during her child-rearing years and has therefore experienced career interruption. Even if she has pursued a career over the years, her focus may have been split between family and work. Now that her children are growing up and need less of her direct attention, she is ready for a reinvestment into her career. After years of nurturing others as a primary thrust in her life, she may be ready to engage more fully in her own career and personal development. Enter the aging parent!

- **Keep your focus on your family**

Clearly, with regard to the family, the middle-aged couple is at a turning point. They are concluding the so-called "launching pad" phase of family life, that is, launching their kids into their own lives and careers, helping them start independent lives and begin families of their own. All this has taken a tremendous amount of resources: financial, emotional, spiritual, etc. It is not surprising that these dedicated parents feel in a state of energy depletion and much in need of rest.

Emotionally, these experiences might be labeled bittersweet, partly because of the "empty nest" syndrome and partly because they are looking at themselves and the future in a new way. There is clear potential for renewal and for "re-coupling" in the middle years; it needs to be pursued with vigor, so the couple can readdress their intimacy needs. Enter the aging parent!

- **Don't neglect your leisure**

  For the middle-aged couple, leisure has taken on a new face. By this time of life, they have arrived at an increased acceptance of themselves. This allows a new sense of freedom and new potential for rebalancing their lifestyle. Formerly, they were living a somewhat lopsided life by primarily focusing on family and/or career. "Making it" in the adult world no longer carries the weight it formerly did. This stage requires a recreating and reenergizing dimension; leisure time activities often can supply this. Enter the aging parent!

  The middle years present opportunities for more serious personal introspection. Adults in their middle years commonly ask themselves: "Is our life turning out the way we wanted it to?" From their new perspective, the idea of time itself seems to be undergoing significant change. Since they are now seeing themselves in the middle of their adult lives, they tend to measure time from two directions: how much has gone by already, and how much is left. This provokes a sense of urgency. Enter the aging parent!

- **Strengthen your faith life**

  Those who study human development at mid-life tell us that people of this age generally begin to sense their own mortality more keenly. For many, this new perspective stimulates a clear deepening of faith. Increasing respect for life, a new reverence for things sacred, and a deepening life of prayer are common surges in the middle years. Faith renewal strengthens resolve and gives added direction to middle-aged adults who now have a new appreciation of life itself. Such reverence encourages a search for self and for soul. Questions commonly emerge around life direction and of living the mystery of faith during these years in much more pointed ways than before. Fruits of this new perspective can be peace of mind and a closer communion with God. Enter the aging parent!

Career, family, leisure, and faith; these four need to be brought into a new balance in the lives of middle-aged adults. Such balance strengthens and upholds you, as you forge ahead with increased caregiving responsibilities.

> *Finding a balance that provides for well-rounded growth is perhaps the best preventive for potential problems in caregiving.*
> *Remember, it is the deep-rooted tree that withstands the hurricane.*

The Parents' Generation

- **Acknowledge the losses your aging parent has experienced, but don't get caught in them**

After looking at the middle-aged group, let us take a look at the same life arenas of their parents' generation. Starting with work or career, we see that retirement—the diminishing of physical strength and other effects of the passing of time—have already introduced revolutionary changes. Sometimes this means that former vocations now become avocations, and vice versa. Oftentimes, it hurts when hard-won practical wisdom and priceless skills learned over a lifetime are shoved to the back of the shelf and ignored. In the vital areas of family and social life, the social circle is drawn smaller and smaller; the nest was emptied long ago; children have moved away; siblings, relatives, old friends, business acquaintances, and many others their own age, are going through similar experiences. Perhaps they have already passed through them.

How do older people view themselves in the elder stage of their lives? They are probably (at least they should be) going through a phase of life called life review. We will get more into this important topic when we cover the Ninth Fundamental Principle of Caregiving.

What seems to increase the most as we age is the amount of disposable time available. Frequently, this increase falls on a person whose physical, emotional, mental, and financial resources are failing. Consequently, much of this time often lacks direction. "What do I do with all of this time?" is a question many elders ask. Nonetheless, the leisure life area remains, for many older persons, a place where they feel useful and productive and thus maintain their sense of self-esteem. Unfortunately, for some elders leisure remains an unexplored territory. This can be especially true for men, who have been almost entirely socialized to identify themselves with their work.

- **Encourage spiritual growth in your aging parents**

The spiritual life has the potential of being a fantastic growth area and reservoir for elders.

Very often, encouragement from their family can stimulate and invigorate this vital arena. You can encourage your aging parent through joint prayer, expressing your feelings on faith; and by including your aging parent in your personal thoughts about how God works in your life.

- **Try to see your relationship with your aging parent as a challenge, not as a clash**

Here we have two groups of people, both of which are in different states of life change. On the one hand, we have middle-aged children who are trying their best to do what is right for their parents. On the other hand, we have aging parents who are trying to live their lives as best as they can and achieve the necessary developmental tasks of their unique life stage. The elder group is experiencing more forced life modifications than at any other time in life, except perhaps at adolescence. These changes usually come at a time of failing resources. The adult children likewise are burdened with new caregiving responsibilities just when they were divesting childcare responsibilities.

The changes in both of these groups set the stage for potential conflict. In the context of such change, a generational clash is almost inevitable. Both groups find themselves in a period of eroding, if not depleted, resources; given a choice, both groups would rather not be faced with the hard decisions they now must encounter. The situation is undoubtedly a challenge for both groups. It is from this vantage point of challenge that the relationship is most profitably addressed. Recognizing the inherent challenge of the situation may save you from regressing into the clashes and generational conflicts that, unfortunately, are all too common.

Three Stories

Described below are three typical stories about what happens when these two worlds clash and come to active or benign conflict, rather than recognizing their respective situations as challenge. Each story brings home a common relationship violation.

- **Be cautious of creating dependence**

The first story is about Janet, Bob, and Bob's mother, Madalyn. Bob's father died about ten years ago. Though widowed and alone (Bob is an only child), Madalyn did quite well in her own home until last year, when she suffered a heart attack. Since then, she has had to sharply curtail her activities, requiring the services of home healthcare and Meals-on-Wheels. Madalyn's physical disability also seemed to bring about a radical change in how she viewed herself. Formerly capable and self-reliant, she became intermittently depressed, as her confidence all but vanished. She appeared incapable of making even the smallest decisions by herself. Janet's phone would ring constantly with requests for Bob to do this or that. Madalyn wasn't interested in talking with her daughter-in-law. She was always asking, even demanding, that her son "be there."

At first Janet was understanding and even compassionate

toward her mother-in-law who had suffered so much. However, over time Janet's initial concern hardened into indifference and even anger. As the requests increased, Bob—devoted son that he was—felt more and more guilty about his own rising feelings of impatience with his mother's ever-increasing demands.

- **Recognize that lopsided relationships either breed guilt and depression, or anger and emotional distance**

The next story is about Rich and Arlene, and Rich's father. From his earliest days, Rich's father meant everything to him. Through his boyhood eyes, there was nothing his dad could not do; Rich idolized his father. Flattered by this adulation, Rich's father seemed to do all he could to perpetuate this "myth." Unfortunately, one of the ways he did this was by criticizing his son: "Rich, you're not doing that right; you don't know how to do things correctly." Even with this constant criticism, Rich continued to idolize his father. Apparently, his own poor self-image was drawing strength from his father's self-assurance and swagger. Meanwhile, Rich's wife, Arlene, realized that this relationship between her husband, now a grown man, and his dominating father was unhealthy; yet, she didn't know what to do about it.

As the biological clock ticked on, Rich's father began to feel the effect of the years. There was a series of minor automobile accidents. Typically, Rich blamed the other drivers. But then others followed, some potentially very serious, that seemed caused by forgetfulness, confusion, or some other bizarre behavior. Even so, Rich wouldn't admit that his "invincible" father was suffering from dementia. Eventually, the weight of evidence pushed aside even Rich's denial. His father's health, stamina, and mental acuity were rapidly disintegrating. What could Rich do? He didn't know how to communicate with his father, because he had never developed an emotional relationship of quality with him. There had been no effort to establish an honest, adult-to-adult friendship; the relationship had been lopsided, with the father holding all the power ever since Rich was a child and, unfortunately, it never was able to grow beyond this.

In time, Rich's father was forced to enter a nursing home. Each time Rich visited his father, he would come away emotionally devastated. Eventually, Rich descended into his own depression, pushed by guilt that he was somehow responsible for his father's condition. Why did he feel such guilt? Why did it seem that it was *his* fault that his father was becoming just a shadow of the man he used to be?

- **Watch for overcommitment, it helps no one**

The final story is about Kay and Steve, and Kay's parents. Kay is a talented, energetic woman with an outgoing personality. She and Steve have no children. Kay has an eighty-three-year-old father as well as an eighty-year-old mother, the latter of whom has Alzheimer's disease. One reason this elder couple are still managing to live in their own home is because Kay does so much for them. She goes there every day, cooks their meals, does the shopping, makes sure they take their medicines, and sees to a thousand other things as the needs arise. Up till now, the strain of what she is doing has not had profoundly negative effects upon her. Yet, the signs and symptoms of this burden are beginning to show. Kay has realized for some time that she has much more to do than she has time for; she is over-committed. Her relationship with Steve is also suffering. She has long discounted her own personal needs. Kay's sense of duty and loyalty drives her to continuously "do" for her parents now that they can no longer fully care for themselves. But cracks are beginning to appear in Kay. We can only hope that, as her parents require increasing care, Kay can create the necessary boundaries needed to restrain herself.

The principal themes of increasing dependence, depression and guilt, and overcommitment portrayed in these three stories are almost universally present to some degree in most adult child/aging parent relationships:

(1) Janet and Bob's story pointed out how the *dependence* of Madalyn kept getting worse and how this affected both Janet and Bob.

(2) Arlene and Rich's story emphasized the one-sided relationship of Rich to his father and how this produced *depression and guilt* in Rich when his idolized father began to show the effects of aging.

(3) Steve and Kay's story was a tale of almost heroic *overcommitment* and the strain this put on all concerned.

Physical Needs

• **Educate yourself about community services**

Like all human beings, older persons have needs that fall into two general categories: 1) physical or material needs, and 2) emotional, psychosocial, or spiritual needs. In the first category, anything that we can see, taste, hear, smell, or touch is a physical or material need. When we lack any of the needs necessary for maintaining life, we have a situation that demands prompt attention. When the family cannot meet the physical needs of one of its family members, there exists an ever-widening network of senior services that can be marshaled. Such programs are organized on several levels: town, city, county, state, and federal. Some specific examples are Meals-on-Wheels, housing for the elderly, heat and utilities allotment programs, transportation programs, nutrition sites, and a number of other programs designed for specialized physical needs. Caregivers need to educate themselves about the nature and scope of these community services. Perhaps the first place to investigate is the information and referral section of your local Area Agency on Aging. Every community in the entire country is covered by these agencies. They are mandated and funded by the federal government to coordinate the services available to elders. Consult your phone book for the AAA listing in your area.

Emotional Needs

- **Regard your aging parent's emotional needs as seriously as you do his/her physical needs**

There are also the emotional, psychological, social, and spiritual needs of older persons. For the sake of simplicity, we will classify all of these as emotional. Are they very important? Recently, a number of influential research studies asked the basic question: "What are the total needs of older persons?" In study after study, right down the line, older persons themselves told researchers that their most pressing needs are not so much physical as emotional. Let us look at some of the most frequently mentioned emotional needs of older persons.

1. *A sense of self-worth.* A sense that I am a human being and that I possess a dignity that deserves respect.
2. *At least one close friend.* This is a central psychosocial need of everyone and especially of older persons. Many research projects have found that the healthiest older people are those who have at least one close confidante.
3. *To feel productive.* The need of feeling productive is an internal sense that "I have the capacity to do. I've done many worthwhile things in my life, overcome many difficulties. I can continue to do that now. I can keep going. I can run my own life."
4. *To feel useful.* Feeling useful is not the same as feeling productive (which is a *self*-affirmation). Feeling useful is an internal feeling generated from the stimulus of outside affirmation, i.e., "There are other people out there who perceive me as a productive and useful member of society, and this perception is recognized and appreciated by me."
5. *To be treated as a unique individual.* To put it negatively, this is the need not to be categorized, not to become a victim of ageism. Ageism, like other "isms" such as racism and sexism, is a destructive prejudice that exists in our society. Its target is any and all who are old.

6. *To possess a meaningful sense of belonging.* "I belong to a group of people with whom I can relate." Often the only group available to some older persons is their own immediate family.
7. *To have control of decision-making.* Free will, the ability to make decisions, is what sets humans apart from animals. This human gift of making decisions should not be denied anyone of any age except for the gravest reasons, as when the person is deranged or comatose.
8. *To overcome loneliness.* One of the most devastating emotional problems older persons are forced to face today is loneliness. Fast on the heels of loneliness is depression, the emotional "common cold" of our society, a sickness to which the elderly are particularly susceptible.

These are the primary emotional needs of older persons. None of us—old or young—has an option to address these needs or to not: They are going to be there. But it is the thesis of this book that something can be done to alleviate their impact: Understanding these needs can help you form appropriate attitudes about them and design strategies to deal with them.

Critical Losses

Losses come into everyone's life. Enumerated below are eight of the most common losses experienced by older people. The list is by no means exhaustive. Think of your aging relatives and identify their own personal losses.

1. Loss of spouse, friends, or family to death
2. Loss of physical mobility
3. Loss of financial security
4. Loss of status in the community
5. Loss of family ties
6. Loss of physical strength and health
7. Loss of self-determination and control over one's own life
8. Loss of self confidence

Adapting to the multiple losses of aging is the primary developmental task that older people must face.

As much as they might want to, younger caregivers cannot buffer elders from suffering these losses; it is part of living on this planet, a part no one can control.

It is easier to handle losses in younger years than in older years. The experiences of older persons are significantly different in that they are irrevocable. They are living in their last phase of life. Younger persons believe they can always do things "later." For older persons, this *is* "later." A loss experienced by an older person, then, is a much more emotionally upsetting event than the same loss would be for a younger person. You can't focus on these losses, and you can't reverse them or take them away: You can't bring spouses back, restore mobility, or provide financial security. So what is left to do? How do you, as a concerned and loving caregiver, keep your own composure and not be so overcome with false guilt that you feel that your own life is being controlled? You cannot deal with the losses themselves, but only with the reactions and emotional responses that older persons give to these losses. Let's take a look at some of the more common emotional reactions to loss.

Have you ever seen an older person who was anxious, fearful, frightened, angry, or even enraged? Have you seen one who was confused, disoriented, maybe not knowing where he or she was? Have you ever seen older persons withdraw into themselves, get depressed, or become paranoid? These are some of the common emotional reactions to loss. Of course, these reactions are not unique to older persons. If you were the one to experience the kind of losses just listed, how would you feel?

Personal Sharing Questions

1. Is your aging parent or relative meeting his/her emotional needs?

   How?

   To what degree are you involved in each of these needs:
   a. A sense of self-worth
   b. At least one close friend
   c. A feeling of being capable and productive
   d. A feeling of being useful
   e. A sense of being treated as a unique person
   f. A sense of belonging
   g. A sense of control in decision-making
   h. A method of overcoming loneliness

2. What losses has your aging parent experienced?

3. What are his/her emotional reactions to these losses?

4. In what ways might you be creating a dependence on you in your caregiving endeavors?

5. How might you become dependent upon your aging parent, relative, or friend?

6. How do your own children impact your caregiving endeavors with your aging parents?

7. What degree of impact has your elder caregiving activities had on your:
   a. work?
   b. family?
   c. leisure?
   d. faith life?

8. To what degree, if any, are you overcommitted?

The Third Fundamental Principle of Caregiving:

❧

Develop a Quality Relationship with Your Aging Parents, Not a Quantity Relationship

A third fundamental care principle is to build a relationship with your aging parent based on quality rather than quantity. The word *relationship* is most important. It takes two people to form and maintain a relationship. Any relationship requires a sense of mutuality and togetherness for it to be successful. Both parties need the nurturance that the other can give. Would it be an adult quality relationship if one person did all the giving and the other all the receiving? No, such a relationship would not be balanced and equitable. You need a balanced, mature relationship with your aging parents. Sometimes, a "one way" relationship is all that circumstances allow, but that isn't the kind of mature relationship you desire.

Lynn's Story

For years Lynn's mom and dad lived ten miles from where she and her husband, Tom, were raising their three children. Now ages twenty-two, nineteen, and sixteen, the two older boys have already moved out of the home. Their teenage daughter, Betsy, has been suspended from high school once and is currently "running around with the wrong crowd."

Into this situation, a new complication entered Lynn's life. Her mother fell and broke her hip. While her mom was in the hospital for three weeks, Lynn invited her dad to move in with them. He had always been a domineering fellow with strong opinions, many of which could even be called chauvinistic. These leanings had already been evident when he retired ten years ago. At that time he could easily have lent a hand around the house, but he chose not to. "Household chores are 'women's work.'" His attitude blossomed anew when Lynn's mom was discharged from the hospital. Her mother's doctor had given her strict orders not to do anything physical for several months. What was Lynn to do? She made a very understandable mistake: She took charge of her parents' household, which had formerly been her mother's domain. But Lynn's biggest mistake was still to come. After her mother had recovered and was able to function fairly well again, Lynn didn't stop her daily visits. She continued her now ingrained ritual of providing on-the-spot service and companionship for her parents.

Deep down Lynn knew what she was doing wasn't good for herself, her family, or her parents, but the truth took a while to dawn on her. After several weeks, however, she could clearly see that she was caught in a dilemma that she herself had created. By this time, her daughter Betsy was heading for real trouble. Tom, her normally good-natured husband, was becoming more irritable every day. Lynn was feeling used, resentful, and angry.

On the other hand, Mom and Dad rather liked what had happened. They continually praised her: "How wonderful, Lynn, that you are coming over to see us; we appreciate this so much." Her father was especially lavish with praise of his daughter. Lynn had to admit she was pleased with this. In the past, she had seldom received affirmation from her father.

Lynn was now locked into a continuous cycle of giving—a cycle that was becoming increasingly destructive to her personal life and to the life of her family. What had gone wrong? Where were her two brothers and her sister, who all lived in town? And, last but not least, what could she do to get herself out of this mess?

• Beware of overcommitment

It is easy to put a name on all this: overcommitment. Overcommitment is by far the most common failing of adult children in their relationships with their aging parents. But when Lynn realized what was happening, why wasn't she able to break away from it? Something deeply psychological was at work here. Unconsciously, she was driven, in a near compulsive manner, to acquire something long past. Lynn's dad had always been more critical than nurturing of her; she never felt that she was fully adequate, wholly worthy. Somehow it seemed like it was all *her* fault, which added a strong sense of guilt to the turmoil she was now experiencing. She had married young, and now as a middle-aged woman she was attempting to retrieve this longed for affection. Catering to every whim of her parents seemed to be the only way she could rid herself of this awful guilt. Little wonder, then, she fell into the trap and was having such a hard time getting out of it.

Why didn't Lynn's brothers and sisters shoulder some of the burden? The answer is rather obvious: What message did Lynn give to them when she said, "Dad, come live with me in my house"? She was communicating that "Dad is my turf; you can stay away." Was that the message she wanted to send? Not at all, but she continued sending similar messages. Her actions kept saying: "I will take care of our parents; you don't have to be involved in this." Her brothers and sister quite naturally reacted: "Let's leave well enough alone. Mom and Dad are being taken care of; why interfere?" All this, of course, had a dramatic impact on Lynn. She felt completely abandoned. She was becoming desperate. By this time, the anger building up in her caused great pain, resentment, and the beginnings of a serious depression.

- **Develop a quality relationship**

How can Lynn get out of this situation? To answer this question, we must take another look at something that was mentioned in the treatment of the Second Fundamental Principle, something called a "quality relationship." Perhaps we can understand what this is if we contrast it with a relationship that is characterized by "quantity" rather than "quality." A "quantity relationship" would be one in which adult children are spending lots of time and energy "doing for" their aging parents; they are doing *many things* for their loved ones.

On the other hand, a "quality relationship" is characterized not so much by "doing" as by "being with" the parent who is now experiencing the effects of old age. A relationship of this type is characterized by a feeling of well-being, experienced both by the aging parent and by the adult child. There's a sense of independence on both sides, no matter what the physical malady or incapacity may be. And always the focus is on the person involved rather than the problem.

The give-and-take of a quality relationship strives for balance. It has a nondirective tone to it, with a special accent on personal growth. We might ask whether Lynn enhanced her father's personal growth by implying that he was not capable of taking care of himself. How different things might have been had Lynn asked: "Dad, what do you think we should do about your living here alone while Mom is in the hospital?" Even better would have been: "Dad, what do you think *you* are going to do when Mom is in the hospital?"

> *Aging parents are best honored by allowing them to tackle their own problems.*

It really wasn't Lynn's problem, but it was her *concern*.

- **Learn what a quality relationship is not**

Let's look at what a quality relationship between an adult child and his or her aging parent is *not*. It is not like the small child/adult parent relationship we all experienced in our early years; both people in a quality relationship are adults. There is, or should be, equality and mutuality built into it. The style of a small child/adult parent relationship is extremely directive. Its goal is to train, guide, and form the little one so that he or she can develop a healthy self-image and thereby be able to handle the multiple relationships that will come in the future. Nor is this a relationship of equality. The parent is right in saying to the child, "I am the parent....I know better....You're the child, so you do what I say." Is that the way we want to be toward our parents? Of course not!

- **A quality relationship is not a supervisor/employee relationship**
Nor is the relationship between an adult child and his or her aging parent like a supervisor/employee relationship. The goal of such a job-related relationship is productivity: "I am the supervisor, I tell you how to get things done." What happens between an adult child and an aging parent should not be like that. Your father or mother is not your employee. Your relationship with him or her is not principally to get things done, even though things have to get done along the way. The style has to mirror the equality that should exist between two adults. Even if your parent is severely afflicted with Alzheimer's disease, your relationship still needs to be one of respect and equality.

Another familiar relationship is that of student to teacher. In most cases this is also very directive in style: "You will do this homework, hand it in tomorrow, and on Friday we are going to have a test." The goal is learning. Adult children are not teachers of their aging parents. Sometimes information has to be given, but it needs to be imparted as directly and as clearly as possible, in a spirit of mutuality. The style of the classroom doesn't "fit" a relationship between adult children and their aging parents.

Relationships

Based on Quality:	Based on Quantity:
1. Being with	1. Doing for
2. Emotional closeness	2. Emotional distance
3. Warm	3. Aloof
4. Fosters independence	4. Fosters dependence
5. Person-focused	5. Problem-focused
6. Feeling-oriented	6. Thing-oriented
7. Mutual equality	7. Dominant/submissive

- **A quality relationship is a "helping relationship"**

A quality relationship is the basis for a helping relationship. To be that, it needs to be characterized by a number of the qualities mentioned. It needs to be as nondirective as possible. In other words, you should not say things like: "You know, Dad, you ought to do this, and if you don't I'm not going to come over any more." A helping relationship means not imposing one's will on the other person. It means allowing your aging parent as much self-direction as possible. This might not be possible with severely sick people, who are demented or suffering from an organic brain syndrome such as Alzheimer's or any other debilitating disorder. Even so, everyone's dignity must be respected.

Ideally, the motivation for establishing and maintaining quality relationships comes from within. Doing things out of a sense of obligation, or because of an undefined feeling of guilt, is not what is needed. Even acting out of a desire to keep others from being disappointed is not a good basis for action: "I must go over, or they will be disappointed." So often we attempt to accomplish the impossible, including controlling the emotional reactions of our own aging parents, in some illusionary attempt to protect them from the "ravages of aging." Disappointment is sometimes unavoidable. It is the other person's own reaction and cannot always be controlled or prevented. Sometimes, all that can be done is to help the other person deal with it. Did Lynn do this? No. Even though Lynn had the best intentions, she nonetheless failed to honor her aging parents. She succeeded in making them more dependent.

So what is a quality helping relationship? Let's look at a closely related question which was part of a study I conducted several years ago. The question was directed to experts in gerontology and administrators of social service agencies nationwide. The question was: "What should our goals be in dealing with the needs of older persons?" Thousands of suggestions came in. They are summarized here in seven headings.

Goals of a Quality Relationship

1. A quality relationship *fosters positive mental health* in your loved one
Positive mental health encompasses these five things:

- emotional adjustment
- ability to make and keep friends
- ability to accept responsibility
- ability to maintain personal independence
- calmness of action

Does your relationship with your parent fit into these categories?

2. A quality relationship *promotes personal effectiveness*
This means that the relationship helps your parent, not only to survive but even to thrive. This suggests that the aging person is encouraged by your actions, not only to maintain a positive self-image but even to be open to future growth.

3. A quality relationship *encourages decision-making*
This means your relationship aids your aging mother or father in identifying and making personal decisions.

4. A quality relationship *expands the knowledge of the aging process*

The way you relate to your parent at this time provides basic knowledge about the physical, emotional, psychological, and social changes that are going on. Because all of us are novices in the business of aging, this information can be very helpful not only for the aging person but also for you, the caregiver.

5. A quality relationship *assists in problem resolution*

There are eight steps to this process:

- briefly state the decision you are thinking about making
- identify the specific problem
- define clearly the decision to be made
- scan your options
- assess the risks and costs of each option
- assess any personal conflicts in each option
- develop a workable plan or strategy
- make the critical decision, that is, solve the problem

To make any decision requires a "leap of faith."

6. A quality relationship *enhances behavioral change*

Change is what living is all about. This holds for the old just as much as for the young. It might even be more important for elders because the losses already experienced demand many changes if the necessary adaptations are to occur. But notice, it says your relationship *enhances* the behavioral changes that your parents make; it does not make these changes for them. To be valid and enduring, the changes have to come from within themselves.

7. A quality relationship *promotes self-advocacy*

The "self" here is your aging loved one. This means that he or she is helped in identifying specific needs and in working toward ways of satisfying these needs. It does *not* mean that you say: "Dad (or Mom), I will satisfy your needs for you; I will become your friend; I will cook all your meals; I will come over every day; I will provide you companionship." It is not your fault that your loved ones are suffering the losses that naturally come with getting old. And if this is true, why is it somehow incumbent upon you to move heaven and earth to satisfy your aging parents' every need?

- **Call a family meeting**

What could Lynn have done to prevent falling into the trap of overcommitment? Planning would have helped greatly. As soon as her mother broke her hip, Lynn should have called a family meeting of her siblings to decide how the situation was to be handled. Together, Lynn and her brothers and sister could have developed a more equitable family response. Certainly, some siblings are better equipped than others to deal with Mom or Dad. Yet, the full force of the responsibility for the aging loved one shouldn't fall on only one adult child: "Let's do this together," is a much better approach. Decisions that are made without input from *all* parties generally backfire.

Characteristics of a Quality Relationship

We have said that a quality relationship has the characteristic of "being with" the aging parent. "Being with" doesn't mean that you are to be physically present all the time. Listed here are three factors you will want to keep in mind when trying to "be with" your loved one in the right way. Think of these as guidelines for helping you to establish a quality relationship.

- **Be yourself...be genuine**

Genuineness is the ability to share of yourself in a manner which is open, natural, sincere, and nondirective. It means to be authentic, to be who you really are, to be yourself. Genuineness includes being open and honest about your own needs. If you aren't—but look only at your parents' needs—you will unwittingly undermine the relationship itself. Was Lynn authentic? No. She was not allowing herself the necessary free-dom of being herself; she was not honoring herself. She was not sharing herself, but rather clutching on to the guilt and resentment she suffered.

There were other problems Lynn was ignoring. She was very worried about her teenage daughter, but she didn't take the time or energy to attend to her; her husband was growing more distant; and she certainly had lost touch with herself. The goal of genuineness is mutual trust, working hard to drop pretense and defense. When you can do that, your aging parent will be more likely to follow suit. Don't sell him or her short. Don't say: "Oh well, Dad never was honest with anybody," or "It is very difficult for Mom to show her feelings." Have you ever tested it out? Have you tried to understand their feelings? Have you told them your own feelings? Maybe they would surprise you. Are you expressing yourself clearly, directly, and with authenticity?

As an example of a genuine response, let's rewrite the exchange between Lynn and her father. He asks her: "Lynn, aren't you coming over today? What will we do for lunch?" A genuine response on the part of Lynn might be something like this: "Dad, I know you and Mom would like me to come over today." (She has acknowledged his needs.) She continues: "I can't come over." (That is clear and direct.) "I love you very much, and I want the best for both of you. I want and need the independence to feel unencumbered by coming over every day. I want you and Mom to be as independent as possible also."

Notice that all sentences started with the word "I." She is not saying, "Dad, you don't need me today; you can fix your own lunch." Nor is she hiding herself in saying, "Gee, Dad, I can't come because I have to take Betsy to the doctor," or "I have other things to do." Such statements are not true! The truth is that Lynn wants a quality relationship; she also wants a break, as well as the same independence for her parents. Her Dad will probably retaliate and ask: "What do you mean, you are not coming over today? What is all this talk about inde-pendence?" But Lynn has done the right thing. She is being genuine. She is expressing her own feelings and thoughts clearly and directly. The word "you" is frequently accusatory. Start your genuine statements with the word "I," and you will receive more understanding and better results.

- **Be compassionate...practice empathy**

Empathy is the second trait of a quality relationship. It is the ability of the adult child to recognize fully what the aging parent is communicating—understand where the aging parent "is" emotionally—and see the world as the aging parent sees it. Empathy is not to be confused with sympathy. Sympathy is used at wakes and funerals: "I am sorry for your loss." Sympathy means that you take your own emotions and express them to the other person for that person's hurt.

Empathy is trying to reflect back what you think a person is feeling or thinking; you are basically restating the communication you have just received.

You are not trying to solve anything; you are not trying to come to any kind of decision. You are simply saying that you understand what has just been said to you. When you're empathetic, you're communicating that you really understand. Very few responses can give such comfort.

Let us look at an example of empathy, again using Lynn's story. Her mother says: "Lynn, you know your father is not one to do for himself. He needs your help. I wish I could do for him now, but I can't." Lynn says: "I know how inadequate you feel since your fall and how hard it is for you to see all the things that Dad needs." Basically, Lynn repeated what her mother had just said to her: "I know how inadequate you feel since your fall." There was some reading between the lines, of course. It is true that Lynn's mom has suffered certain losses since the fall; she is no longer mobile; she can't do all she used to; she feels inadequate. Lynn says to her: "I know how you feel, Mom." Then she follows that up by acknowledging that it is particularly distressing for her mom not to be able to fulfill all of her dad's needs. What is her mom's response going to be if Lynn said something like: "I know how inadequate you feel, and I know it is hard for you not to be able to do for Dad like you used to"? Her mother might well respond: "You are right, Lynn, it *is* hard." Lynn is "with" her; she is emotionally "there." The bond between Lynn and her mother will be stronger, and her mother will think better of her daughter; she will respect Lynn. Lynn is probably doing the best thing she can with such a statement. It is much more important than vacuuming the living room or fixing an egg salad sandwich.

- **Be care-ful...always show respect**

    Unconditional positive regard, or respect, is the third characteristic of a quality relationship. It is an attitude that accepts the right of the aging parent to think and feel the way he or she wishes. It is saying, in effect: "Hey, it's okay. It is not the way I do things, but if you want to do things that way, that's fine with me. I am not going to make you live according to my standards, because my standards are different from yours. I am going to let you know what my opinions or ideas are, but you are the master of your own universe. You do what you think is right." In such statements there are no hints of judgment, criticism, or disapproval; there is no arguing, threatening, ridiculing, rejecting, and belittling. You give affirmation and acceptance.

    Let's look at Lynn's story again, and see how it could have exemplified respect. Her father says: "Lynn, you know you never come by the way you used to." That is clearly a loaded statement. What is being said is: "You'd better start coming over." Lynn could interpret this statement as a threat. She could say something back like: "You have no right to say that to me." I know some adult children who would say exactly that to their parents: "Don't you know I have a life of my own? Don't you know I have things to do in my life? When you were my age, you weren't encumbered by stuff like this." That adult child is going to walk out of that house and think: "Why did I say that? What am I doing? This is not the way I want to react to my parents; this is not the way I want to react to anybody; but I am doing it. This is crazy."

Suppose Lynn would say something like: "It sounds like you want me to come over more often. I know that you feel I need to be there more often. I respect your position on that, and I hope you can respect mine." Is she being clear and direct? Yes. So many times, our communications with our adult parents are muddled and hazy.

> *In the final analysis, our only goal with our aging parents is to love them.*

We honor them by loving them. But this love has to be shown. The road to expressed love is the road of a quality relationship. A quality relationship is not cheap or quick. It is not shallow, nor is it easy. It takes work! This principle provides you with a path leading to a quality relationship. The path is sometimes rocky and hilly, but it leads to a land of honor, a land where peace and harmony prevail in an atmosphere made confident and bright by the light of the Spirit.

Personal Sharing Questions

1. To what degree is your relationship with your aging parent or relative a "doing for" relationship rather than a "being with" relationship?
2. To what degree is your relationship with him or her a:

   a. *student-teacher relationship?*
   b. *employee-supervisor relationship?*
   c. *child-parent relationship?*

3. What could you be doing now to *help* your aging parent or relative?

   a. *fostering positive mental health*
   b. *promoting personal effectiveness*

  c. encouraging decision-making
  d. expanding knowledge of the aging process
  e. assisting in problem resolution
  f. enhancing behavioral change
  g. promoting self-advocacy

4. Formulate a *genuine* response to your aging parent if he/she were to say to you: "I want you and your brother (sister) to promise me that you will never put me in a nursing home."
5. Formulate an *empathic* response to your aging parent if he or she were to say to you: "When your father (mother) was alive things like this never happened!"
6. Formulate a *respectful* response to your aging parent if he or she were to say to you: "You never come by the way you used to."

THE FOURTH FUNDAMENTAL PRINCIPLE OF CAREGIVING:

❧

There Are Very Few "Right" Ways or "Wrong" Ways to Care for Your Aging Parents. Rather, It Is Mostly a Matter of Informed Decision-making, Based on the Best Information Available at the Time

- **Analyze your attitudes about aging**

    Your personal attitude about aging in general, probably more than anything else, colors the way you deal with your aging parents. Because of that, this chapter opens with a little quiz. The purpose is to bring to the surface some of the underlying assumptions and attitudes people have about aging. The following fourteen questions are to be answered with a simple "yes" or "no." Try to answer them with *all* older persons in mind, not just your own aging parents:

    1. Are old people narrow-minded?
    2. Do old people worry about unimportant things?
    3. Do old people feel sorry for themselves?
    4. Do old people live mainly in the past?
    5. Are old people stubborn?
    6. Is it true that old people cannot manage their own affairs?
    7. Are old people cranky and irritable?

8. Do old people like to be waited on?
9. Do old people feel depressed most of the time?
10. Are old people bad patients when they are ill?
11. Are old people boring?
12. Are old people untidy and careless about their appearance?
13. Is it true old people cannot concentrate even on simple tasks?
14. Are old people unable to acquire new knowledge?

Since you were asked to respond with either a "yes" or a "no," your answer probably reflected how you read the question at the moment. It is my opinion that for each of these questions a "no" is closer to the truth than a "yes." I say that for several reasons. First, the questions are too sweeping and all-embracing. They seem to be asking about *all* old people, and are accusing the whole group of possessing some unattractive trait or exhibiting some negative behavior *all the time*. We know that isn't true. Many people who are of advanced years by the calendar don't show this pattern at all. Moreover, all of these behaviors can be seen in some people who are decades away from "old age." None is the exclusive property of elders.

- **Recognize that what you sometimes see as aging is *not* caused by the aging process at all**

  Another basic reason is that the questions imply that the particular trait or behavior is the result of the aging process itself. For example, question number seven suggests that an old person is cranky *because* he or she is old. The truth is that a person is cranky because something has happened to him or her. This something—probably one of the losses referred to under the Third Fundamental Principle—has no intrinsic or direct connection with growing old. It can happen to anyone at any time. Whenever it happens, whether to young or old, it always provokes some emotional reaction.

*Your aging parents may exhibit crankiness, stub-
bornness, or any other of these negative traits, but
aging itself has not produced them.*

Some other event, situation, personal history, or physical
process has been at work: An emotion or strong feeling is
involved. It is important to realize that aging is as much an
emotional process as it is a physical one.

- **Older persons are as intelligent as younger ones**

Fortunately, that was not the only testing done in this area.
More recent research has come up with the following: There
are some areas of intelligence where older people decline very
slowly. The ability to recall quickly seems to decline after age
fifty, but only imperceptibly so. However, while intelligence
can be measured in terms of productivity, it can also be measured in terms of exercising a level of caution. Older persons
may not have to reinvent the wheel because they have experience. They already know how to do this or that. The safety
record of older workers, for instance, is much better than the
safety record of younger workers. These items are clear measures of intelligence. All things being equal, older persons are
no less intelligent than are younger persons. Sometimes,
unfortunately, we think they are because we've got some problems with understanding the aging process itself. But these problems are ours. We are holding on to some unfounded assumptions about "old age." We have to revise our stereotypic view
of those we consider "over the hill." Unless we can do that, we
will never be able to establish a healthy relationship with our
own aged loved ones.

Hillary's Story

Let's look at an example of an adult child who suffers from
an attitudinal distortion about older persons. Hillary is an
attractive forty-eight-year-old woman who is active and
fun-loving. She has always enjoyed herself and the people

around her, is fun to be with, and has always been the life of any party she has gone to. She plays racquetball weekly and jogs two miles every day. Hillary's mother was much the same as Hillary when she was younger. As a matter of fact, Hillary and her seventy-three-year-old mom have, in the past, enjoyed many active times together. However, over the past two years Hillary has begun avoiding her mom. They used to meet every week for lunch, and have a long walk afterward. This became much more intermittent as Hillary's mom requested that the walks become shorter: She was slowing down, normally and naturally. When compared to most people her age, she was probably in better physical shape than most. Hillary's avoidance of her, however, was actually an attempt to escape or deny her own aging. She was unable to reconcile in her mind the idea of aging in its normal and natural consequences with the fact that her mother, and eventually she herself, would face these physical losses. Hillary didn't want to get older. Her attitude about aging, and especially the specter of her own aging, was distorted and consequently very dysfunctional for her as a daughter. It was certainly damaging her relationship with her mother.

We Become More Different Over Time

Perhaps the premier principle for a caregiver to keep in mind is:

As we mature, we become more different—not less different—from everyone else.

One way we can conceive of this is to imagine two groups of people in a large room. Those on one side of the room are all eighty years old, while those on the other side are twenty. If their age was the only fact you knew about these two groups, about which group could you make the most generalizations? The answer is: the younger group. The aging process makes people *more* unlike other people as they progress through it.

- **Your aging parent cannot be accurately compared to other older persons**

Since older persons cannot be categorized into one homogeneous group, this presents you, as a concerned adult child caregiver, with a very challenging task. Your own parent, grandparent, relative, or friend is very much an individual. His or her genetic makeup, physical condition, personality, temperament, history, and view of life, is as different as night and day from other people of the same generation. Every word, gesture, sigh, frown, or smile is as characteristic of that person as is his or her fingerprints.

Stereotypes and "Myths"

There are other attitudinal problems that frequently interfere with healthy relationships. These are sometimes called "stereotypes" and sometimes—incorrectly—"myths" and, as such, they are often used interchangeably in popular literature. A stereotype is a rigid, standardized perception about a category of people or things. In its derivative—"popular"— meaning, a myth is a false belief about something.

There are many examples of this type of thinking. Let's look at the case of Harry. Harry's father had just celebrated his sixty-fifth birthday and had retired from a thirty-year position the same week. Harry himself was busy climbing the ladder of success and, up to this point, would eagerly share his successes and his business triumphs with his dad. Somehow, after his father's retirement, Harry seemed to change in the way that he related to his dad. The relationship grew somewhat distant and strained. What had disturbed his formerly happy relationship with his father was a "myth" that Harry had "bought into" many years ago. Without being the slightest bit aware of what was going on, Harry had always harbored the false belief that men were only men if they worked, if they were somehow productive.

• **Age is only a number**

Sixty-five is our culture's normal retirement age. Unfortunately, that in itself is a "myth" created in 1873. Bismarck, who was then chancellor of the new Germany, took a look at all the graphs and charts on longevity of life and realized that only about three percent of the people lived beyond their sixty-fifth year. Bismarck wanted to be looked upon as a very forward looking leader, so he instituted, with a great fanfare, his equivalent of a social security or pension welfare system. This was the first time that any government had ever done that. He knew if he graphed sixty-five as the time that people would start receiving benefits he'd be paying out very few benefits because, at that time, longevity was not much beyond that age. Today, longevity has gone much beyond that; yet we are stuck with sixty-five as the beginning of "old age."

This chronological marker is really very silly, and potentially harmful, because it may become a self-fulfilling prophecy for becoming old. In any event, since sixty-five is our culture's normal retirement age, Harry equated that age with nonproductivity, nongrowth, and generally a self-depreciating kind of posture. Harry couldn't associate himself with such negativism. His own stereotypic ideas about retirement, growing older, and the watershed age of sixty-five inhibited him from rejoicing in the newfound lifestyle that his father was experiencing. This is a prime example of how false perceptions and stereotypes can impair the way you relate to your aging parent.

Some persons have the idea that old age is a period of constant decline and decay. Only rarely are some of the positive things that may come with aging looked at: the wisdom, experience, and mellowness that can emerge in one's later years. In other cultures age is revered, but in our culture we seem to do the opposite: Somehow being young is seen as an accomplishment in itself. Why is that, when actually the opposite is true? How did we get that way?

- **We can learn new things until the day we leave this earth**

One prevalent perception is the idea that older people can't learn new things. As the saying goes: "You can't teach an old dog new tricks." Many of us have this statement working somewhere down deep in us, and we may actually believe that it is true. To test this hypothesis, IBM once did an interesting study. They identified a group of workers, aged fifty-five and older, whom they wanted to retrain. Then they compared this group to people they were retraining who were age thirty-five and under. Lo and behold, they found no differences in their ability to learn and to apply their learning. The educators who did the training reported the older people to be the better students; they did their homework and paid better attention. That says something very positive about aging.

People can improve at any age if they want to, provided they are surrounded by people who recognize that and encourage them. But if they are surrounded by people who believe all sorts of stereotypes and false opinions about elders, then older persons will not improve but become dependent.

> *The most damaging thing about false beliefs and stereotypes is precisely that older people themselves start believing them.*

"Gee; I'm sixty-seven. I've got the 'disease' of old age. I'll start slowing down because society tells me I'm supposed to slow down. Because that's what a sixty-seven-year-old is supposed to do, I guess I will." This is what we call a self-fulfilling prophecy. It happens "just because" we believe it. We really do live in our own realities, and our own realities are derived from our own thinking more than anything. Changing our thinking is what we are striving for—changing the realities we hold between our ears.

- **Examine your attitudes for traces of ageism**

Earlier in this book mention was made of a thing called

"ageism." This is a very destructive prejudice which generates discriminating behavior against older people simply because they are older. It consists of stereotypes and beliefs that are, at best, half-truths and poorly founded assumptions. We have become very sensitized in our culture to other prejudices and "isms." Racism and sexism are two prime examples. Very few people would fail to react if someone came up and said: "This particular race is more intelligent than that race"; we would all recognize this as a racist statement. Again, if someone said: "Women's place is in the home and that's where they need to stay," this is clearly a sexist statement.

We are just beginning to get sensitized to ageism. "Don't worry about it, he's kind of old. We can't do much for him. Just let him sit there. It is all right. He's seventy-three, you know." Such ageist statements are as ravaging to any person's dignity as a racist statement or a sexist statement would be. As a society, we still subscribe to much of what ageism preaches. In itself, the very fact that our society is getting older will help solve a lot of these problems. Meanwhile, we have this notion in our society that some sociologists have referred to as the YAVIS syndrome. The YAVIS syndrome states that all of us would rather deal with people who are "Young, Attractive, Verbal, Intelligent, and Successful." Anybody else, somehow, is not quite up to standard; growing older certainly doesn't measure up. To what degree is the YAVIS syndrome within us? We have to examine ourselves.

- **Learn to reframe illogical thinking**

One disturbing observation that I have made time and again with adult children is of their illogical thinking about aging in general and the aging of their own parents in particular. Our thoughts rocket through our brains and determine to a large degree how we, mentally and emotionally, will process the entire caregiving endeavor with our aging parents. Thoughts find their expression in our feelings, and our feelings always find expression somehow, either internally through sickness, or externally through irritability, anger, frustration, and the like. Our thinking is the fountain from which flows our feelings, our decisions, and finally our actions. Our thoughts form the basis for our evaluations of ourselves, our aging parents, and the ways we deal with both. Examining our thinking pays us handsome dividends. I've assembled here ten of the most common thought distortions that I recognize as the most damaging. Examine each and determine to what degree each may be "at work" within you.

1. I will not tolerate change in my aging parent

> *Like many an illogical thought, this appears silly when we examine it "in the light of day." Yet how many of us do not look with a sad disdain on any change that we notice in our parents which seems somehow related to their aging? Physical changes, mental changes, ability changes, and the like are generally met with sadness or anger or both, even by well-meaning adult children. To what degree do you allow your aging parent to age?*

2. My aging parent doesn't do enough to help him or herself

> *"Why doesn't she get more exercise?" "Why doesn't she socialize more?" "Why doesn't she eat better.... follow her doctor's instruction better....hold a conversation better....walk better....talk better....smile more....?" The common denominator in all these is that they are illusions: they deny reality, they are illogical.*

3. My aging parent should be more kind and understanding of me

> *Here's another example of the illogical thought, above, when applied to one's own feelings. Many adult children actually feel abused by their aging*

parents. Of course, in some cases this is true. Yet, what is most often termed "abuse" are the negative feelings that so many adult children caregivers experience. These feelings are the result of illogical thinking, but it is so easy to see our parent as the one who has "imposed" these negative feelings upon us. The truth, of course, is that we imposed them on ourselves.

4. I should feel only positively toward my aging parent

The Fourth Commandment instructs us to honor our aging parents, and we are commanded to love them. However, this is not a command to like them. This is a real distinction—one that needs to be heeded. You may readily agree this thought is illogical; but why is it that when we do have feelings of guilt, anger, sadness, anxiety, fear, etc., about our loved ones, we emotionally scramble ourselves further by feeling badly about the "bad" feelings we have about them? The reason is that we, in fact, do believe this illogical thought, and we use it against ourselves frequently.

5. I must obey my parent

In our formative childhood years, we needed to obey our parents. We usually did what they wanted simply because they said it was the right thing to do. Now, many years later, that urge to honor their requests—to obey them—still lurks deep within us. Yet, who among us would intentionally do something that is obviously unhealthy or hurtful to our aging parents simply because they said we should obey them? Once again, this sounds absurd, but it can cause havoc in our hearts.

6. I must find solutions to all situations involving my aging parent

> *How ridiculous a thought. However, I find armies of adult children caregivers acting as though this statement were true. They mercilessly punish themselves into thinking that they are the solution of last resort for their aging parents, that they must "fix" it all. Some adult children even seem to think that they can "fix" aging itself.*

7. I'm at fault when things go wrong

> *I find it incredible that honest and responsible adults—who are able to differentiate responsibility in every other area of their lives—seem to shrink from logic when it comes to their aging parent, and go on to shoulder all the "blame" for something that happens to him or her.*

8. I'm not doing a good job with my aging parent

> *Here is one of the consequences of pursuing a "quantity" relationship, wherein you feel responsible for everything regarding your aging parent. When you see yourself as the provider of your parent's every need, when something does go wrong—as it most certainly will—you blame yourself as if the situation is testimony to your inadequacy. This "knee jerk" reaction becomes compulsively overpowering for some adult children caregivers.*

9. I'm the one, perhaps the only one, that really knows what's best for my aging parent

> *"Only I know how to bring Mom to the doctor." "Only I can fix Dad's eggs the way he likes." "Only I have the power to bring order and harmony into our parents' lives." On and on goes this illogical way of thinking. Again, it is not ever expressed directly in words, but actions speak louder than words. I encourage you to examine your actions toward your aging parents, rather than what you say to them or about them.*

10. I can never do enough for my aging parent(s)

> *Here is a real obsessive way of thinking. I've encountered adult child caregivers who find it difficult to think about much else except their aging parents. The responsibilities and strains of caregiving have overburdened them to such a degree that the caregiving has invaded their thinking, leaving room for little else.*

Personal Sharing Questions

1. Identify some personal attitudes about older persons that may hinder your relationship with them.
2. What (if any) false beliefs did/do you hold about older persons?
3. To what degree are you prejudiced against older persons; to what degree are you ageist?
4. What personality characteristics do you remember about your parents from childhood that might act as barriers today in dealing effectively with your aging parent?
5. To what degree should/can you shoulder the caregiving relationship for your parent(s)? Describe.

6. Which of the ten illogical thoughts about aging and caregiving most "hit home" with you? Which ones do you think you need to modify? Describe.

The Fifth Fundamental Principle of Caregiving:

❧

Establish Boundaries with Your Aging Parents in Order to Love and Honor Them as Completely as Possible

Specific Problems of Adult Children Caregivers

The fourth principle offered a general backdrop against which we can project a fifth principle. It deals with the specific problems and challenges that you have as caregiver to your own parents. You have to deal with the various *general* beliefs and stereotypes about aging. You also have another whole set that is uniquely your own: You are your parents' child; you were integrated into a specific developmental setting called a family; over the years, you have established a unique relationship with your parents. They were your primary sources or resources of learning how to deal with the outside world.

> *The way you—consciously or subconsciously—perceive how your parents cared for you when you were young has a tremendous impact on your caring behaviors with them today.*

Your father was the primary person from whom you learned how to deal with the males in your life. Your mother, your primary female influence, taught you how to relate with other females regardless of your own gender. Furthermore, in their interaction between themselves, your parents served as the premier model of how to relate with all others as well. What you were taught here has become part of your personality. That's why you need to get "in touch" with your past.

You need to understand how you feel about the way you grew up, and what you now want or need from your parents. Some of this is hard to deal with because it is very deep and psychological. If your home was a battleground, filled with bickering, fighting, and criticism, how will you find yourself dealing with your aging parents now?

What assumptions are you making about your parents? There will always be some assumptions and viewpoints from your childhood—some ideas and attitudes from the past— which are still influencing you. You need to identify and clarify them. To the degree that these deep-seated controlling feelings remain unrecognized, you may be fighting yourself unnecessarily as you care for your aging parent. Neither you nor your parent needs a resentful, anxious, or depressed adult child.

Georgia's Story

Georgia is the second of seven children. Very early, she and her older sister were called upon to shoulder a large portion of the care for their younger brothers and sisters. This was especially so after her mother became ill. Her father was a rather active entrepreneur who enjoyed traveling, making business deals, and fraternizing with his friends down on the corner. His responsibility to the family generally ended with bringing home the paycheck. Georgia's interaction with her father centered around childcare responsibilities and getting household chores done. Consequently, Georgia eagerly wanted out of her home. She got married at the age of nineteen and began a family of her own. Now forty-four, her relationship with her father is very complicated. On the one hand, she desires her father's recognition, his attention, and his love—something she feels she never got while growing up. On the other hand, she feels slighted and deprived by her father, and harbors deep personal resentment and anger about all of this deprivation. The result is that Georgia is almost emotionally paralyzed when interacting with her father: She wants a relationship, and yet somehow also wants to "even the balance" for the inconsistencies and the injustices she feels were a result of her father's domineering and critical attitude during her childhood.

Fortunately, Georgia was able to find a counselor who could help her sort through these family issues so she didn't allow her negative feelings to intensify. She has been able to recognize the unconscious revenge she harbored against her father, and she has been able to dispose of it through learning what and how to forgive. In this way, she has formed a vehicle both to honor her father and heal herself.

Types of Caregivers

All caregivers are not the same; they are called to do different things in different ways. Decide what kind of caregiver you are currently called to be.

1. Active Caregivers: Those who perform direct services such as medical support, food preparation, and the like.
2. Support Caregivers: Those who give assistance to the primary, active caregiver through home maintenance, financial support, emotional support, and the like. Support caregivers offer care to the primary caregiver.
3. Distance Caregivers: Those who live outside the area of the aging parent and yet offer supportive care from that distance, either to the elder or to the primary caregiver.
4. Management Caregivers: Those who perform very few, if any, direct services, but who see their primary function as one of arranging, administering, and accounting for caregiving services.

Many Levels of Care

- **Decide the level of care you are prepared to give**

As there are different types of caregivers, there are many different levels of need required by aging parents. Generally, it is a progression of care that is needed; as the aging process continues its relentless march, care requirements increase. At first, only minimal care is required: checking in on the elder, more frequent phone calls, monitoring their situation, etc. As time passes, however, more involvement is generally required: shopping, transportation, food preparation, medical support, etc. When and if the time comes for moving into an assisted care facility—a place where usually one meal is provided as well as minimal recreational activities—care does not end; it simply moves to a different level. Finally, when complete skilled care is required, the caregiver's level of involvement needs to shift again. Now that physical and medical care is provided, other kinds of care—emotional, psychological, familial, and spiritual—emerge as most pressing.

- **Learn how to selectively say "no"**

Why do so many adult children have such a difficult time saying "no" to their aging parent? Somehow, deep within there is a pulsating feeling that if they say "no," they will pay a horrible price for it. What could be that horrible price? One of the prices could be the withdrawal of parental love. This person, their own parent, has given so much to them; therefore, the adult child owes this much or more in return.

When you were a small child, perhaps a two- or three-year-old, your parents were like demigods to you. Their word was law; they were like two giants towering above you; their love for you provided the emotional sustenance needed to nurture you. Even though you were very young, you implicitly knew you needed their love. When you felt their love, you felt secure and safe. When you were disciplined, and they temporarily appeared to withdraw their love from you, your world suddenly became hostile and fearsome. If you lost the love of you parents, you would suffer an emotional death.

This sense of impending doom from way back then can still be felt today. If you lose your parents' love, your unconscious mind fears that you just might suffer an emotional death. "If you don't eat your dinner, you are going to be sent to bed," amounted to "I'm not going to love you if you don't do the things I want you to do." That tape was recorded time and again, in your very depths. What do you think is playing back to the adult child now, in the relationship with the parent?

Sue's Story

Sue is a fifty-two-year-old mother of three girls, two of whom are now out of the home. She works full-time and is a loving spouse to her husband, Harry. Her mother, Helen, now eighty years old, has lived alone in a housing unit since her husband (Sue's father) died ten years ago. Helen rarely goes outside except to go to the corner grocery store—a short distance she is quite capable of walking. Recently, however, Helen began to ask her daughter to do her grocery shopping for her. At first, her request was for a few small items to "carry her over." Now, she is asking Sue to get all her groceries for her. Should Sue grant her mother's request? refuse? take some middle ground between these two? How would Sue best honor her mother here?

For Sue to shoulder the full burden of grocery shopping for her mother, when she is fully capable of doing it herself, would produce an unhealthy result. Sue's mom would become increasingly dependent. As the dependency deepened, as it inevitably does, Sue's mother would become increasingly unhappy, and most likely physically unhealthy as well.

- **It is OK to say "no" to your aging parent**
  I remember a sign I received from a friend when our children were teenagers: "What part of 'no' don't you understand?" I posted the sign on the refrigerator for our children to see.

They needed to know that they couldn't magically have all that they wanted; they needed to know that there are boundaries in life. Life without boundaries becomes a frightful place indeed. Children need boundaries; boundaries give them the security of knowing that there is a higher power, there are right and wrong, there is "organization" some place. Children will push their parents until they find boundaries. If they find none, they become exasperated, and prone to all sorts of "acting out" behavior, because they lack the security of boundaries.

As children need boundaries, so do we all. This applies to our aging parents, as well as it does to ourselves. Many times, I find that some taboo seems to lurk in the minds of some adult children who, for some unknown reason, believe they can't set boundaries for their parents. They believe that saying "no" sets boundaries. "No" is a very kind word: it lets the other person know, proof positive, what you will and will not do for him or her. Your aging parents need to hear this kind word from you at times. They need boundaries. They need to know what you will and will not do, what is appropriate and what is not. Without the word "no," you are not in control of yourself, and the relationship between you and your parents is guaranteed to be shallow and unsatisfying.

The right course of action for Sue would be to say "no" to her mom. This may sound cruel to some people; after all, hasn't Sue's mom done enough grocery shopping in her life? What's wrong with doing a little shopping to help her out? "What's wrong" is that taking over an activity of daily living before it is necessary, even at their request, is doing a disservice to any elder. Sue taking over such an activity would hamper her mother's ability to satisfy one of her primary human growth needs—that of "feeling useful." Sue's mother's request is probably motivated by something quite different from groceries; it is this "something else" that we must try to uncover and clarify.

Where might you need to say "no" to your aging parent?

Where might you need to step in with an unpopular decision in order to honor your aging parent more fully?

- **Watch out for guilt**

The fear of withdrawal of love can generate other feelings, such as rejection, punishment, and an overriding guilt: "I feel so guilty when I say 'no.' How can I say 'no'?" I have counseled people who are convinced that they can't break out of this "trap" that confines them to always conceding to the wishes of their aging parent. I believe they can break out, but they choose not to because they are unwilling to face the tremendous weight of guilt their conscience would burden them with if they do. What motivates such an incapacitation? At the very base of this insecurity is a paralyzing psychological fear: the fear of not living up to expectations. Has this happened to you? Even if these expectations become rather distorted and burdening as your parents get older, you still want to satisfy them because you want their love and approval.

- **Could you be practicing "reaction formation"?**

Sometimes, the reason you don't say "no" is because you are secretly angry; you use what is known as "reaction formation" as a defense. Suppose you are inwardly angry, with an anger that is too scary for you to bring up to a conscious level. You say to yourself: "I shouldn't be angry at my mother." Anger is a mature human emotion which most, if not all, adults experience from time to time. Anger itself is not the problem; the problem is repressing the anger, and then having it emerge in a form that is unhealthy for you, and perhaps for others as well. So you go through an unconscious psychological process called reaction formation. You are not even aware you are doing it. It allows you to think: "I'm not angry with you; I love you."

This can happen between you and your aging parent as a result of some of the uncertainties and insecurities you feel due to all the discipline, the structure, even perhaps the sense of unfairness you felt as a child: "Make sure you get an A. Got to get A's in school. I want you to lead the class. I want you to play tennis like a pro. You've got to play football." All these demands and expectations made up so much of our relationship with our parents that, way down deep, we may resent them. Different parents give them in different measures.

- **Develop a caregiving game plan**

  Here are six ideas to help you avoid the obstacles that prevent you from having a quality relationship with your aging parent:

1. Get as much knowledge about aging as you possibly can. In this case, knowledge is power. When you have an understanding of the aging process, you will have power to address issues with confidence.
2. Clarify your relationship with your parents as it exists now, and compare it to what formerly existed when you were young. How do you recall your parents' behavior? Do you recall them being caring and loving; were they critical, judgmental, domineering, and authoritarian; or was it somewhere in-between? Most relationships with parents are somewhere in the middle. Parents aren't perfect. Many children feel that their parents tread on them. To some degree, that still may be working against you.
3. Establish your caregiving boundaries. Determine how much you can give. How much can you give without putting an undue strain on your relationship with your mate, your kids, or your God? Where do you draw the line? There is no simple, clear-cut answer. I can't tell you where to draw the line, and no one else can either; it is clearly your considered choice. This is a personal and familial judgment, and the only way you can make a good judgment is to have knowledge about the aging process. It is important to clarify where you are in your relationship with your own parents.
4. When you recognize that your parents need something or some service that goes beyond your ability or is outside your

caregiving "game plan," find substitutes—other people or agencies that can provide the needed service. We are living in an increasingly service-oriented society, and there are many people who can help you: home healthcare agencies, Meals-on-Wheels, friendly caregiver visitors, and many church programs. Don't feel guilty about getting substitutes; they may be able to do it better than you. Your parent doesn't have to "play parent" to them, as he or she does with you.

5. Become clear and direct in your communication with your parents. You will learn much more about this in the next principle, which deals with communication. The interaction most adult children have with their parents is not clear and direct. There are many subtleties present, and that leaves a wide range for misinterpretation, both on the part of the parent and on the part of the adult child. "What did she really mean by that?"

6. Most important: Take a step back. Recognize that you are not the "happiness provider" for your aging parents. Your aging parents must live their own lives. Maybe the way they are living their lives is not the way you would want them to, but it is their life. Nowhere is it written that you have an obligation to change their lifestyle. Honoring your aging parents has much more to do with accepting and support-ing them than it does with trying to change them. We have this idea—"Well, I'm her daughter/son, so I can really com-municate with her"—which is a fallacy. Someone who is much more objective can usually communicate better than we can. That is why there are professional people like psy-chologists and counselors and clergy. Use the helpers that are available to you.

Personal Sharing Questions

1. How do you set boundaries when dealing with your aging parent?
2. To what degree did you see yourself in Georgia's story? Describe.

3. What type of caregiver are you: active, support, distance, or management?
4. How, and to what degree, does "guilt" enter into your caregiving endeavor?
5. Write your caregiving "game plan."

THE SIXTH FUNDAMENTAL
PRINCIPLE OF CAREGIVING:

∽

*Simple and Direct Communication
Is Your Strongest Caregiving Tool.
There Are No Shortcuts, Tricks, Gimmicks,
Trendy Techniques, or Easy Solutions*

- **There are no easy answers! (Sorry)**

Clearly, there are no simple solutions. There will not be a time when you can say, "I've now completely figured it all out!"

> *Dealing with your aging parent, relative, or friend could continue to be one of the most frustrating problems that you will ever encounter, yet potentially a most beautiful one.*

Trying to do the "right" thing with your aging mom or dad can be like dealing with an adolescent son or daughter. In fact, built-in psychological snags, left over from your childhood, can sometimes confound your relationship with your aging parent. This can happen to such a extent that your frustration level is raised even higher than what it was (or perhaps still is) with your own teenager. But does that mean it is all hopeless? Our job in life is to address the issues, however difficult, that we have been given. Your parents clearly fit into this category.

• **Develop and stick to quality communication techniques**

An essential element of every successful relationship between an adult child and an aging parent is good communication. Communication is at the heart of any genuine relationship. In your relationship with your aging loved one, you are not there to handle finances, although handling finances may be part of the problem. You are not there to vacuum the living room rug, although periodically that may be part of it as well. You are not there to provide "happines" for your aging parent. You are there to honor your parent, and that means to enjoy a quality relationship with him or her. Our goal, at this point, is to look at communication.

> *Quality communication is the beating heart of a quality relationship.*

• **Learn to listen actively**

Active listening means more than not speaking: It means to discern the full meaning of what your aging parent is trying to tell you. This is not easy. The speech patterns of some older persons are sometimes muddled, shaded, and consequently difficult to understand at times. Active listening means that you are patient, and you wait for the full message to come through. When actively listening, you always ask yourself the internal question: "What is she really trying to say? What's his message?"

Active listening establishes trust. A certain lack of trust can develop between an adult child and an aging parent. This can be carried to an extreme, producing high levels of suspiciousness and even paranoia. If this has happened in your situation, you would no doubt welcome some good news. It is not an exaggeration to state that this lack of trust can be practically eliminated by learning and becoming adept at "active listening." Nor is that the only good thing that will happen.

Self-esteem improves once you allow a person to self-disclose and to express his or her feelings. By actively listening, you are automatically raising your aging parent's self-esteem. When we listed the basic human needs of older persons in the treatment of the second principle, one of the first was raising self-esteem. Moreover, active listening gives you the opportunity to understand your parent more fully. How can you genuinely know him or her if you don't listen? Using this skill also gives your parents a chance to clarify their ideas, their thoughts, and their feelings.

Another need outlined in the Second Fundamental Principle was the need to find solutions to problems, that is, to establish problem-solving patterns that will help your parents make decisions on their own. Active listening is the first step toward achieving this goal.

These are some of the things that active listening can do. What is involved in this skill, and how does a person acquire it? It is more than merely not talking, although being silent at times is certainly part of it. Sometimes that's the problem. Silence is difficult for most of us.

- **Learn that silence can be your friend**

A professor told this story about one of his students. He received a call one afternoon from a young man who said: "I'd like to come over and talk with you." The professor agreed. The student came over and sat down in the professor's office. The first five minutes went by and the student didn't say anything. The professor didn't say anything either. Ten minutes went by, fifteen minutes went by, thirty minutes went by, and still nothing was said. Not one word between the two individuals was exchanged. Then the student got up and left. Two weeks later, the professor got a call from the student saying: "I want to thank you so much for all you did for me that afternoon. You really helped me a lot."

Actually, that professor did help the student. He had no need to fill up that afternoon with words the student obviously didn't need. Much, however, was communicated in that silence. He communicated respect, understanding, and concern. He was giving to that student exactly what was needed:

time in the presence of a caring, understanding person of authority perhaps, or of a father figure; time simply "to be." Perhaps this is what your aging parents need, too. They need simply "to be."

Attending to Your Aging Parent

If real communication is to occur, a certain intensity of presence is demanded. But this presence—this "being with" another person—is impossible without attending. Attending seems so simple a concept to grasp that you might wonder why it is mentioned at all. As simple as attending is, it is amazing how often people fail to attend to one another.

- **Type One attending: physical attending**

Your body plays a large part in your communication. You should adopt a posture of involvement in your interactions with your aging loved one. The basic elements of *physical attending* can be recalled through the help of the acronym SOLER:

> S *-face the person Squarely. This posture says "I'm available to you."*
> O *-adopt an Open posture. Crossed arms and legs are at least minimal signs of lessened involvement.*
> L *-Lean toward the other. This is another sign of availability or presence.*
> E *-maintain good Eye contact. Look directly at the person you are speaking with.*
> R *-be relatively Relaxed. This says "I'm at home with you."*

This lineup is not meant to be followed in any rigid way. Attending should serve the communication process; it is not an end in itself. The important thing to learn is that your body *does* communicate for good or ill.

- **Type Two attending: psychological attending**

If you are constantly delivering messages with your body, the same is true for your aging parent. He or she is also sending many bodily messages of which you should be aware. When you are tuned in to these messages, you are using *psychological attending*. This means you are alert to both nonverbal behavior (such as gestures and facial expressions) and what is called paralinguistic behavior (such as tone of voice, inflections, spacing of words, emphases, and pauses). It has been shown that the nonverbal and paralinguistic cues can contradict the surface meaning of the words. For example, tone of voice can indicate that a verbal "no" is really a "yes."

One of the ways to become an active listener is to use what are called "subtle encouragements" in your communication. These subtle encouragements can take many forms. Small responses, such as "um-hum," "I understand," nods of the head, and repeating the last words that your parent just said to you, are all excellent examples of encouragement to talk. Your mother may say: "Gee, I think I would like to go shopping." A good response might be simply to say, "Go shopping?" It sounds awkward when explained, but when it is actually done it becomes not at all unnatural. This says to your parent: "I'd like to hear more about this." Many times we cut people short; there might be a lot more that they want to say.

- **Get out of the judging and criticizing "business"**

Another important skill you can put to good use in dealing with your aging parent is nonjudgmental behavior. It appears that we have a lot of *shoulds* and *oughts* in us. A well-known psychologist, Albert Ellis, maintains that all this "shoulding" is very abusive. Sometimes it is very subtle, as in: "You know, Mother, I think you ought to get more exercise." Your mother may need more exercise; her doctor has probably told her to get more exercise, but there is an implicit judgment or criticism in that statement. How will it most likely be received? With resistance! People usually respond with resistance whenever unsolicited advice or criticism is given. Such resistance may show up as a tendency, on the part of many aging parents, to do exactly the opposite of what you'd suggest.

> *Nonjudgmental behavior means learning to suspend your own evaluation in deference to your parents' opinion.*

They may be wrong, and you may know that they are wrong. As long as this mistake is not health-threatening, your job is to "let it go." If your mother is eighty and she hasn't exercised for sixty-five years, what makes you think she's going to start now? Judgmental behavior only drives you and your aging parent apart.

Maria and Mrs. S

What follows is a dialogue which we will use as a case study. It is a conversation between Mrs. S and her daughter Maria. Maria says,

> "Hi, Mom. How are you doing today?"
> "Oh, not too good today," responds her mother.
> "What's wrong?"
> "I'm just so dragged out; I can't seem to get going," sighs her mother.
> Maria says, "Well, you shouldn't spend so much time watching TV. If you got a little exercise, like the doctor suggested, you wouldn't feel so tired all the time."
> "Oh, what does he know."
> "Well, anybody could see you need to get up and get around. You don't go down to the senior citizen's center like I want you to. You refuse to invite people in, for fear they will criticize you. You're just sitting here slowly dying. How do you think that makes me feel?"

"I just wish I could be around when you get older."

"Oh, you are just depressed because nobody calls you anymore."

"They do so call; they just can't come over."

"Mom, you know that's not true. You just won't look at reality anymore. What's the matter with you? Are you taking all the medication your doctor prescribed? I'll just bet you aren't."

Mrs. S, holding back tears, says, "Maria, why are you so hard on me?"

"I'm not being hard; you just think I am because you're not doing what you know is right."

Mrs. S, who is now crying, says, "I try, Maria, I try."

Maria, now moved with guilt, says, "Now, now, Mother, it is all right. You are going to be just fine."

"Do you think so, Maria?"

"I'm sure of it. Just do what the doctor and I tell you. If you'll do that, you'll be fine."

What went wrong here? Why did this conversation degenerate, first into a verbal battle and then into an exercise of seeing who could lay the most guilt on the other? Well, for one thing, Maria gave unsolicited advice. As mentioned, most people don't want advice, and that seems to be especially true of older people. If you do that with your aging parents, you will find that they have probably thought of all the things you're suggesting anyway. Their problem is uniquely theirs, and the solution you devise will be uniquely yours and probably nonfunctional for them. One of Maria's statements was, "You shouldn't spend so much time watching TV." Notice the *should* statement in there. Even if these words were said in a benign and caring way, they still have all sorts of negative overtones. First, it implies incapability. Second, it sets up an authoritarian relationship. Without realizing it, Maria was asserting, "I'm the boss, and you are the child." Third, if Mrs. S really wanted advice, she'd ask for it. Fourth, advice is always given from your own point of view, and it usually doesn't take your aging parent's perspective into consideration.

What else did Maria do wrong? She analyzed and interpreted Mrs. S's words with statements like, "You're just sitting around here slowly dying" or "Oh, you are just depressed because no one calls you anymore." Such analyses are inherently disrespectful, even when they are not meant to be. Next, Maria's statement, "You just won't look at reality anymore," was critical and unnecessary. Another remark by Maria, "You're not doing what you know is right," is also off the mark. Isn't Maria really saying "You're not doing what *I* think is right"? Besides, most amateur analyses and interpretations are incorrect. Research has shown that interpretations rarely, if ever, change behaviors. No wonder Maria's approach didn't work.

The next thing that Maria did was to offer her mother false reassurance. There is a place for reassurance. It is when you know beyond a doubt that the situation is going to turn out the way you portray it. But to say things like, "Don't worry, everything is going to be all right" or "This will all pass and you'll be your old self again soon," is damaging because it is only a temporary fix. Maria didn't really know what was going to happen. Improvement of her mother's health may or may not be in the future. Even though a younger person may believe that things will get better because they always seem to, the same idea does not necessarily apply to an older person. With elders, it is more likely that the situation will not improve. We might want to deny this fact. I've heard family members talk to people whom they know are terminally sick and be so fearful of the impending death that they completely deny it. The nephew, for example, who says: "Don't worry, Uncle Fred, next week you're going to be out fishing again." Since it is much more probable that Uncle Fred is going to die soon, it is not at all reassuring to tell him he's going to be fishing next week. Uncle Fred needs to confront his death, not deny it.

Maria reacted strongly to her mother's statement: "I'm not feeling too well." What rose up in her was anger. She wasn't sure why she felt that way, so she reacted instead of thinking: "Okay, I'm feeling some anger here, but I'm not going to let this anger interfere with how I should act." She first expressed this anger at her mother, and then, as soon as her mother began to cry, she felt guilty. Acting out of guilt is another way to dishonor your aging parent. Maria allowed this feeling of guilt to take over. It made her falsely reassure her mother. This scenario has probably repeated itself many times. False reassurance engenders dependence. What Maria was basically saying was, "You can't think for yourself, so I'll think for you."

Maria is really a very nice person. Unfortunately, she fell into many traps that were part of the situation. With other people, Maria is just wonderful; it is only with her mother that she has a problem. What would have been a better approach?

- **Learn the communication skill of exploration**

The first skill she could have exercised is "active listening." There is another, related skill, which also would have served Maria well: a process skill known as "exploration." Exploration means to identify the facts that can bring meaning to a confused person or situation. How is it done? As a caregiver, you need to develop these three abilities:

- **clarify issues**
- **recognize problems**
- **establish life goals**

Beyond active listening, Maria needed to do some exploring. Maria could have helped matters a great deal if she had searched for the *exact* meaning of her mother's words. For example, when Mrs. S said that she didn't feel "too good today," what was she really trying to say? Was it, "I'm really not doing well at all"? If this was her meaning, was she referring to not feeling well emotionally or to not feeling well physically? There is a great deal of vagueness in her statement. This is where the skill of "making concrete" is very important.

- **Use the communication skill of concreteness**

    One of my jobs in the hospital where I worked was teaching physicians. As interns, they learn how important it is to search out any facts that may have a bearing upon the condition of their patient. For example, suppose you came to your physician and said: "Doctor, yesterday I didn't feel very well." If your doctor did nothing but hand you a piece of paper and said, "Here's a prescription. I want you to take these three times a day," what would you think? Since he didn't find out any of the details of the sickness—if it had an onset two weeks ago or only yesterday, whether the condition was acute or chronic—how could he diagnose it properly and suggest the correct treatment? His mistake was that he was not *concrete*. He didn't make it specific enough.

    Let's apply this to your conversation with your aging parent. In trying to discover the meaning of a statement, you must continually strive for "concreteness." If you don't concretize things your parent says to you, how can you be helpful? In Maria's case, what was the true meaning behind her mother's statement about not feeling well? Was her meaning, "I don't know what to do to help myself"? Was it that she was confused? How many different interpretations could there be for Mrs. S's statement? When Mrs. S said, "Oh, what does he know," referring to her doctor, was she expressing difficulty in following his instructions? Was it an expression of anger at her physician—and maybe at herself?

> *You can never be absolutely sure of what your aging parent is trying to say. That is why the effort to make things as concrete and as exact as possible is so important.*

- **Refine the communication skill of accurate empathy**

Another skill of good communication is called "accurate empathy." Basically, this means expressing that you understand what others are saying or feeling; that you are "walking in their shoes," so to speak. You need to communicate empathy to your parents. Accurate empathy isn't difficult to do; it just takes some practice and alertness. Restate what your parents said. You can tack in front of your restatement a phrase like, "You mean…" or "Mom, I didn't quite understand what you meant when you said…" or "Could you help me out? What are you really saying here?" This is what I call peeling the artichoke of feelings until you finally discover its heart.

This sounds simple, but it could have a profound effect on your relationship. Of course, it has to be done on a consistent basis. Positive results will not materialize overnight; however, in time you will notice a real difference. This may be confusing to your aging parent at first, so you may want to introduce it gradually. Over time, its benefits will become obvious to all.

- **Become like a communications mirror**

This next communication skill is an adjunct to the skill of empathy and is called "reflection of feelings" or "response to feelings." The following table is a list of "feeling" words arranged in a very special way. In the left column are seven basic feelings. These are: happy, sad, warm, angry, cold, confused, and weak. You will notice that there are three levels of intensity: weak, mild, and strong. None of these words is foreign to you. They are the most powerful words you can say to your aging parent. I implore you to sprinkle your conversations with them because they will give you power (in the good sense of that word), and they will also empower your loved one.

How do you use them? Let's take a look. Feelings are the movers of the drama of life. Everything we do is motivated by a feeling. The driving force behind our feelings is our thoughts. Feelings drive our behavior. When we clarify our feelings, we

FEELINGS LIST

INTENSITY FEELING	WEAK	MILD	STRONG
HAPPY	glad fortunate contented	joyful great up	ecstatic overjoyed joyous
SAD	cheerless somber unhappy	melancholy dejected downcast	dismal sorrowful gloomy
WARM	sunny alive responsive	affectionate close cordial	passionate fervent enthusiastic
ANGRY	mad frustrated sore	disgusted irritated inflamed	infuriated incensed enraged
COLD	ungracious sassy cool	discourteous impolite indifferent	imprudent vulgar abusive
CONFUSED	unsure embarrassed uncomfortable	flustered muddled mixed-up	bewildered trapped perplexed
WEAK	decayed spent broken down	impotent frail withered	shattered powerless exhausted

are necessarily clarifying our thoughts. Many of us have not learned how to express our feelings, but feelings are a measure of the warmth, emotional responsiveness, and attentiveness in a relationship. Unfortunately, many of us have not had a good education in identifying feelings. Fortunately, we can learn.

When you are talking with your parent, try to become like a mirror. Hold that mirror up to what your parent is saying. Let it reflect back the thoughts, the attitudes, and, most importantly, the feelings expressed by your aging parent. Every single word is weighted with feeling.

> *The person who's best at picking out those feelings and reflecting them back is the person who can build the most quality into the adult child/aging parent relationship.*

This is a simple yet profound statement; a statement which can pay marvelous dividends in enriching your relationship. The positive results that you will be able to achieve with the skill of reflection of feelings will amaze you.

Some Examples

Let's look at some examples. An eighty-one-year-old woman lives in an extended-care facility. She says: "One day just seems to mesh into another. They don't seem to be separate or distinct like they used to be." Perhaps your parent has said something like that. How do you respond? Do you say: "You shouldn't think that way. Look at the sun, it's shining. Before you know it, the robins are going to be here and the crocuses are going to be up; it really is a nice day, don't you think?"

Another way to respond would be: "Mom, it sounds to me like you're feeling kind of gloomy today because your days seem to mesh into one another." Why is that a better response? For two reasons: One, you have identified a feeling and you've reflected it back—you have used the mirror of your mind; two, you also have reflected back some of the content that she said to you. You may think that this is a simplistic, even a depressing way to respond to your mother. I can assure you, however, that a response like this will enrich the very heart of your relationship. It can also protect you from getting caught in the web of guilt—the feeling that it is somehow your fault that your mother is feeling so badly. Ultimately, responses such as these can prevent you from creating a dependent relationship.

Remember, you don't have to find solutions. You don't have to give advice. You don't have to ask, "Why don't you do this?" or reprimand, "You shouldn't feel that way because...." Forget controlling behavior. Your aging parent is in the last segment of life. After your parent dies, you don't want to have to ask yourself: "Did I handle this right; did I do that right?" If you are trying to "be with" your loved one in mind and heart, you're doing the right thing.

A seventy-seven-year-old man says: "I don't want to go to the hospital—those doctors don't know what they're doing; I'll never come out of there." You know that he's got an abdominal aneurysm and needs surgery, and, if he doesn't get it he will die. Your helpful and caring response could be something like: "You feel enraged that you have to go into the hospital. You're also very worried about the outcome of the surgery the doctors have recommended." You don't say: "I'm sure those doctors know what they're doing," or "Well, don't worry about it because, you know, my uncle went in for the same exact operation you need. He's fine today. He's doing great." Maybe you want to get to that later, but first this man needs to get his anger out. He needs to express his worries. Let him do it. Let him get these emotions out into the open. That's what he needs. That's how you can be most helpful to him at this point. Eventually, as the conversation progresses, you might get to your uncle who had his abdominal aneurysm repaired with great results. But to get to that before you get to this man's feelings would be doing him a disservice and would be robbing you of a potential quality relationship with him.

Focus on Feelings

You have a choice when you communicate with your aging parent. You can focus primarily on the content of what is being said, or you can expand your focus to include the feelings behind the statements. If you focus on content alone, you will find the relationship somehow lacking, shallow, and relatively unfulfilling. By focusing on feelings, however, you give life to your interactions, zest to your conversations, and most importantly of all, you add quality to your relationship and honor to your aging parent and yourself.

This Sixth Fundamental Principle outlines a simple, sequential procedure you can follow to enhance your communication with your aging parent. That sequence is:

1) Exercise active listening. Demonstrate your interest in what is being said.

2) Be open to what is said. Do not judge, evaluate, or analyze; remain nonjudgmental.

3) Make sure you know what your aging parent is saying. Try to understand the real meaning of the communication; help your parent to be as concrete as possible.

4) Identify the feelings motivating your aging parent to make this statement.

5) Recognize, and communicate back, an affirming reason why your aging parent feels the way he or she does.

This five-step procedure can be summarized as follows. Suggested "response leads" are included.

1. Active listening
2. Attending posture
3. Clarify meaning; be concrete
   a. "You mean..."
   b. "I hear you saying..."

c. "Could I check this out..."

d. "Help me understand. You're saying..."

4. Identify the motivating feelings
    a. "You feel..."
    b. "So you're feeling..."
    c. "It must be difficult for you to feel so..."
    d. "How do you feel about that?"

5. Give an affirming and understanding reason for the feeling
    a. You feel _____ because _____.
    b. I wonder if you're feeling _____ because _____.
    c. Could it be you feel _____ because _____?
    d. Your feeling of _____ is under-
    standable to me since _____.

Personal Sharing Questions

Now you have an outline and description of good communication. This can help you honor your aging parent. Successful communication leads to a maximum level of honor! Practice your new skills on the following cases:

1. A seventy-one-year-old widower says to his oldest son: "Your
   brother hasn't called me for a month."

2. A seventy-four-year-old mother, calling from her apartment:
   "You'd better not come to get me today for dinner. I'm just
   feeling too low to come over." (Said to you the morning of
   the family celebration which has been planned for some
   time.)

3. An eighty-year-old father, calling from a resident care facility: "There is no one to talk to around here; no one cares. I
   want to go home!"

4. A seventy-eight-year-old mother, living at home with her
   husband: "Your father is getting so irritable. Either he sits
   in front of the TV or he gets angry at me."

5. An eighty-three-year-old mother, three years after death of
   her spouse: "I'm so tired. I just want to die."

THE SEVENTH FUNDAMENTAL PRINCIPLE OF CAREGIVING:

❧

Caregiving Offers You Many Opportunities for Profound Personal Learning in the Classroom Called Life

Caregiving to elders can be one of the most personally instructive endeavors we undertake. As we delve more deeply into the caregiving process, we learn about ourselves, our elders, and about life itself. When we blend our faith together with the immediate life experience of caregiving, what emerges is wisdom and inspiration: wisdom generated by life experience, and inspiration generated by faith experience.

- **Find joy in your caregiving**

  We are all called to discover the joy in our lives; how often did Christ instruct us to "be of good cheer"? There is a lot of potential joy in caregiving once we come to appreciate the vitalizing "life curriculum" that it offers. The "strain of care," outlined earlier, is dismissed by joy. Joy and stress are opposites; when we feel joy, we don't feel stress. Joy does not mean that we continuously feel "warm fuzzies"; nor does it mean that we see only delight and hyper-enthusiastic excitement all the time. Joy is much deeper than that; joy is knowing that God is with us always.

Joy helps us suspend our petty judgments. We find that we experience fewer "shoulds," "oughts," and "musts." With joy, we learn to withhold criticism and condemnation. Joyfully, we're able to surmount our doubts; we feel connected, filled-up with life, and whole with God. Joy is giving love and finding forgiveness. Joy is not only possible in the caregiving situation. It becomes a goal for us. Over time, we successively learn to become "joy-finders" rather than "fault-finders." We learn to become "joy-givers" rather than self-absorbed "fun-seekers." Caregivers who grow toward wholeness find that they take care of themselves best by giving joy.

- **Transform your damaging caregiving attitudes**

Another means for personal growth that is offered by caregiving is the transforming of our attitudes. Each of us has beliefs about ourselves and about caregiving. In a sense, caregiving is a slice of living; as we learn more about caregiving, we are simultaneously learning more about ourselves and about life in general. Beliefs and attitudes are the foundational ideas that direct our living; they determine how much joy or sorrow, happiness or sadness, delight or dejection we will experience in our lives. Our attitudes are the keys to a successful life.

Caregiving forces us to clarify our attitudes, sometimes challenge our attitudes, and even transform our attitudes. Through my experience with hundreds (if not thousands) of elder-caregivers, I have been fortunate to identify attitudes that can cause the most havoc in the emotional life of a caregiver. These turmoil-producing attitudes I term "guerilla attitudes" because they execute hit-and-run fighting tactics. Guerilla fighters are known for their stealthiness; they usually attack unnoticed in the dark of the night. We don't even discover the damage they have wrought until morning breaks. Guerilla attitudes conduct similar "attacks" on the "peace-of-mind" in our dark recesses; we don't even know the damage that has been done until we find ourselves feeling depressed and guilty, anxious, and forlorn. Many a caregiver has walked a long road of guilt due to not clearly having identified these dangerous attitudes, and consequently being unable to work toward transforming them.

The Ten Guerilla Attitudes That Emotionally Terrorize Us

Each of the following ten destructive guerilla attitudes is followed by its enlightened version. The enlightened version represents the personal life learning that can be derived from the caregiving role. As you can see, the enlightened attitudes are not simply applicable to the caregiving situation; they are attitudes of wisdom, helping us to live more authentically, genuinely, happily, and joyfully!

Damaging Attitude Number One: "I need my parent's approval to make me feel good about me."

Enlightened Attitude Number One: "I am full and complete just the way I am; there is no lack within me."

So many of us suffer from extreme approval-seeking behavior. Caregivers seem to be particularly susceptible to this malady, probably due to their unusually high levels of sensitivity. So often, caregivers give endlessly. Somewhere in their caregiving, they do expect some "payback," usually in the form of gratitude or appreciation from their aging parent. When this appreciation is not forthcoming, caregivers can emotionally discount themselves. This internal self-depreciation can cause self-blame, and also push caregivers to blame and judge their aging parent as well. Neither of these is emotionally healthy.

Damaging Attitude Number Two: "I can very easily feel guilty."

Enlightened Attitude Number Two: "I achieve inner peace through forgiveness."

Guilt seems to be all but universal among elder-caregivers. When we use guilt as our motivator, we do damage to the health of any adult/adult relationship. Jesus taught us that love is the primary motivational force. We have been given a marvelous tool which we can use against guilt: forgiveness. Forgiveness is the process of letting go of the need for guilt as a motivational factor in our lives. We all make mistakes; in fact, our mistakes are what defines us as human. The caregiving situation can be our teacher, giving us instruction on how we can come to overlook our mistakes, the wrongs we may have committed. The Eighth Fundamental Principle of Caregiving covers this in detail.

> *Damaging Attitude Number Three: "I need peace at any price."*

> *Enlightened Attitude Number Three: "Conflict exists in the world; I cannot control it."*

Conflict can be found in all adult/adult relationships; it is a fact of human existence. Our job is not to avoid conflict by adopting a "peace at any price" posture. Our job in life, regardless of the relationship, is to allow a conflict to bring the two parties closer together. A "peace at any price" attitude insures that the relationship will not be truthful. Truth requires honesty, forthrightness, and candor. Our only obligation with our aging parents is truthfully to state our feelings and beliefs as clearly as possible. When we try to control the behaviors of others, or even "stuff" our own feelings, we wind up in turmoil.

> *Damaging Attitude Number Four: "I'm the victim of this caregiving situation; I'm always in the middle trying to please everyone."*

> *Enlightened Attitude Number Four: "I am not a victim of the situation; my perception is my choice."*

When we see ourselves as victims, we feel like a cork being tossed around in an unfriendly sea. When we take on the role of victim, we ensure that we will be unhappy. What thoughts rocket through you, for example, when your aging mother calls and asks: "Why didn't you call me last night?" When you see yourself as a victim—held hostage by the caregiving role—the almost automatic internal reaction might be: "Can't I even have one night off from you?" Such a thought is like a guerilla fighter, or a stealth bomber, damaging your emotional countenance. Substitute the word "learner" for the word "victim"; when you do, the tremendous emotional burden that you sometimes feel begins to lighten.

> *Damaging Attitude Number Five: "If I'm not super-responsible, then I'm not worthy."*

> *Enlightened Attitude Number Five: "I am worthy just because of who I am, not because of what I do."*

So many times, caregivers feel that love and approval will be withdrawn if they don't "measure-up." Such a feeling of conditional love and approval doesn't simply come from their aging parent, but also from themselves. Caregivers can blame and judge themselves if they feel they don't "measure-up" to some unreasonable, perfectionistic standard. Such thinking is from our psychological "inner child," certainly not from us as responsible adults! The goal is an adult/adult relationship, where worthiness doesn't have to be earned; it simply is. You are a child of God. There is no higher status in the universe. You didn't have to do anything to achieve this exalted status.

> *Damaging Attitude Number Six: "I feel so sorry for my aging parents."*

> *Enlightened Attitude Number Six: "I have faith that there is a reason and purpose for aging; aging is part of God's divine plan."*

Feeling sorry for anyone who is aging (and that includes most of us) is perhaps the most emotionally damaging feeling we can have. When we feel sorry, we automatically think that somebody needs to do something about this aging process. We find ourselves fighting aging itself, as well as all the people who won't "help" aging. This attitude is covered in depth by the Tenth Fundamental Principle of Caregiving.

> *Damaging Attitude Number Seven: "Only I can help my aging parent."*
>
> *Enlightened Attitude Number Seven: "I am part of a caregiving team which wants the very best for my aging parent."*

Caregivers are not omnipotent; they are not super-people. Learn to see yourself as part of a team of caregivers. Seek to assemble others: family members, friends, relatives, volunteers, and professionals whose combined efforts and expertise can converge upon your aging parents, thereby creating a safety-net of enlightened services. "Going it alone" almost always creates emotional turmoil, if not outright caregiving disasters!

> *Damaging Attitude Number Eight: "I can't stand to see my aging parents angry or resentful; they need to (should) be calm and at peace."*
>
> *Enlightened Attitude Number Eight: "My aging parents, today, are the way they were when they were younger, only more so!"*

Your aging parents, like everyone else, developed their own personalities. The factors that influenced their personalities most include: biology, family background, education, and all manner of life experiences. You were—and are—not responsible for any of these. One's personality is a very stable, psychological foundation, and it doesn't change much over the years unless there is some biological insult at work. Aging can push a personality to its limits, and when this happens the "flaws" that seemed very small in the past become magnified. We must remember that what we see as negative emotions or reactions are sometimes the very responses that protect your aging parent from experiencing even more damaging emotional trials. For example, anger is commonly "used" by older persons as a cover-up for depression. If they didn't protect themselves with anger, they would subject themselves to the darkness of depression.

Our personalities seem to become somewhat exaggerated as we mature; little idiosyncracies in earlier life may become bigger and bigger as we mature. The way people respond to life—how they handle "the slings and arrows of outrageous fortune"—pushes them in quite divergent directions. There are more differences, sharper distinctions, and more dissimilarities among an older population of people than in a younger population. Like deepening wrinkles, individual personality styles intensify with aging. Each older person is unique, a son or daughter of God unlike any other; each requires a different style of care.

> *Damaging Attitude Number Nine: "I can fix, or should be able to find a solution for, any of my aging parent's problems."*

> *Enlightened Attitude Number Nine: "Only things can be fixed; people are healed, but only if they want to be."*

When you place yourself on the pedestal of the "all-powerful adult," you are setting yourself up for failure. The bare fact is that you cannot "fix" your aging parent. You cannot arrange his or her life in such a way that all will go smoothly. People cannot be fixed—they are healed, but they cannot be healed with an unwilling heart. We simply cannot control the emotions of another. We cannot create a perfect world for our aging parents; it's an illusion.

Damaging Attitude Number Ten: "I can (should) do it all."

Enlightened Attitude Number Ten: "Today I choose only peace."

There is always more to do; more can always be done. Many adult children who are caregivers try to keep everything as it was when Mom or Dad was hardy and healthy. They scamper about, trying to keep everything in place, to arrange for any eventuality, and to protect their aging parents from any and all consequences. This is a formula for stress of the highest order. This is a formula for quick "burnout."

These ten damaging attitudes rest in deep places within you; you may not even be aware of them at all until they rear their heads and cause you pain and distress. I encourage you to examine your heart, to search for them and others like them. They can bring you to your caregiving knees.

I encourage you, however, to move your focus away from the guerilla attitudes and on to the enlightened attitudes. These potentially life-transforming messages can gain you a confidence which will eventually lead to invaluable life-learning. Make no mistake about it: Just as your parents taught you when you were young, they teach you still today. Take advantage of this "life curriculum" that God is providing for you.

Personal Sharing Questions

1. How much joy do you experience in your caregiving? Describe.
2. Look at each of the ten "guerilla attitudes" that terrorize caregivers; rate each on a scale from 1 to 10, with a response of "1" meaning that you have not been bothered by this at all, and a response of "10" indicating that this attitude has greatly interfered with your caregiving.

Guerilla Attitudes:

Damaging Attitude Number One: "I need my parent's approval to make me feel good about me."
 1 2 3 4 5 6 7 8 9 10
does not bother me   bothers me a lot

Damaging Attitude Number Two: "I can very easily feel guilty."
 1 2 3 4 5 6 7 8 9 10
does not bother me   bothers me a lot

Damaging Attitude Number Three: "I need peace at any price."
 1 2 3 4 5 6 7 8 9 10
does not bother me   bothers me a lot

Damaging Attitude Number Four: "I'm the victim of this caregiving situation; I'm always in the middle trying to please everyone."
 1 2 3 4 5 6 7 8 9 10
does not bother me   bothers me a lot

Damaging Attitude Number Five: "If I'm not super-responsible, then I'm not worthy."
 1 2 3 4 5 6 7 8 9 10
does not bother me   bothers me a lot

Damaging Attitude Number Six: "I feel so sorry for my aging parents."
 1 2 3 4 5 6 7 8 9 10
does not bother me   bothers me a lot

Damaging Attitude Number Seven: "Only I can help my aging parent."
 1 2 3 4 5 6 7 8 9 10
does not bother me   bothers me a lot

Damaging Attitude Number Eight: "I can't stand to see my aging parents angry or resentful; they need to (should) be calm and at peace."

    1   2   3   4   5   6   7   8   9   10
does not bother me   bothers me a lot

Damaging Attitude Number Nine: "I can fix, or should be able to find a solution for, any of my aging parent's problems."

    1   2   3   4   5   6   7   8   9   10
does not bother me   bothers me a lot

Damaging Attitude Number Ten: "I can (should) do it all."

    1   2   3   4   5   6   7   8   9   10
does not bother me   bothers me a lot

THE EIGHTH FUNDAMENTAL PRINCIPLE OF CAREGIVING:

～⚬～

*Creative Acceptance— "Letting Go"—
Is Your Most Valuable Ally
for Peace of Mind*

Recently, a very insightful elder-caregiver gave me pause to think as she expressed her thoughts and feelings regarding how to deal with her aging mother, who lives alone some forty miles away. Her initial statements outlined what she called the "craziness" of approaching her caregiving responsibilities in exactly the same way as she always had. She said she was making the same mistake over and over again. She didn't exactly know what that mistake was, but she was open to exploring possibilities.

She explained that she needed to look at her mother and her caregiving role with "new eyes." This was not a denial of reality, she reasoned, but indeed a means of perceiving reality more clearly and accurately than she had—to be more accepting of what was true. She wanted to do things in a different way, adopt a new sense of what she termed "yielding," because the way she was running her life was simply not working. What she related seemed to be giving greater definition—and certainly practical meaning—to a whole new notion, one I have come to call "creative acceptance."

Creative Acceptance

Other caregivers expanded on creative acceptance. They used words like surrender, distancing, disengagement, non-interference, letting go, and "letting it be." Together, all of these give us an enriched understanding of a process whereby we can maintain ourselves by perceiving the events of our lives differently. As we perceive differently, eventually we feel, decide, and act in ways more in keeping with objective reality.

The obvious theme running through acceptance is underscored by the fact that we need to exercise faith so we can transcend our worldly reality and discover a new reality: a spiritual reality. We can certainly point to the power of prayer as our vehicle for transcending the mortality of this physical plane and accepting the mystery of the next plane. Other virtues frequently mentioned by caregivers, both as paths to acceptance and areas of character and spiritual development are: patience, tolerance, forgiveness, understanding, and courage. Each of these provides us with a slightly different tool necessary to construct the bridge from caregiving anxiety to caregiving acceptance.

- **Embrace creative acceptance not as submission or defeat, but as triumph**

Caregivers are quick to point out that moving from a posture of control to one of acceptance is not tantamount to defeat; indeed, the contrary is true. They regard this transformation as a challenge. They find this nonresistant stance of creative acceptance to be in harmony with the central learning task of aging: developing integrity. This brand of integrity speaks to wholeness, completeness, and cohesiveness as opposed to fragmentation, separateness, and brokenness.

Control begets illness and loss of self, whereas acceptance fosters health and self-preservation.

Acceptance confers a power to handle the conflicting negative emotions that the caregiving role often brings.

Creative acceptance demands a live-in-the-present attitude, which is implicitly positive in its perspective. Once experienced, it is seen as natural and normal rather than artificial and awkward. Acceptance brings with it an inner peace, an internal calm which feels like a piece of heaven; it is comforting and affirming, trusting and loving. Creative acceptance seems in concert with that spark of the divine which glows within all of us, regardless of how lost or clouded we may feel.

Creative acceptance helps us to transcend the dread that we are somehow losing something as a consequence of our caregiving role. Acceptance helps us see what we have gained through our caregiving. When we perceive caregiving as a loss, it engenders a split mind and necessarily brings strident resistance and emotional turmoil. Viewing caregiving as a learning process—and therefore as a path toward growing and gaining—enables us to be in harmony with God's will for us.

Creative acceptance is not a state of being; it is a process of becoming. Acceptance is an ideal; we can never completely achieve it, but we can grow closer and closer to it. We are not called to attain perfect acceptance. We are merely called to accept it as our goal!

- **Commit to seeing things differently, take a different view**

Caregivers often perceive that the problems they encounter are caused by their aging parents. "If my aging parents would only see the illogic of their thinking and the logic of mine." One of the first steps of creative acceptance is to "own" the problem as ours rather than theirs. In so doing, we can claim the problem as a vehicle for our own growth; a challenge for personal development.

Acceptance is identified by caregivers as their number one need. When we stop and evaluate our situation, isn't it acceptance that could genuinely extricate us from the angst we sometimes feel about our attempts to "honor" our aging parents through our caregiving responsibilities? Do we really accept their decisions, feelings, history, and imperfections? To find happiness in the caregiving situation, we need to fully accept the reality of aging, its consequences on our parents as well as on ourselves. We need to accept our existential helplessness in the face of the realities of aging and the human condition.

- **Find the peace that creative acceptance brings**

It is curious to note the striking paradox in the philosophy underlying various Twelve Step programs. The foundational first step is to admit having no power whatsoever over one's addiction. How can claiming powerlessness actually help the addict grow through, and eventually triumph over, the disasterous effects of his or her abuse? One would contrarily think that by rendering ourselves powerless we would fall deeper into the grips of the addiction! Such is not the case. This is analogous to the caregiver situation. By some curious mental mechanism, when we admit to our inherent powerlessness to change our aging parent and/or the aging process—indeed, when we let go of our attempts at controlling—we discover that we can transcend our "doomed" attempts at seeking solutions to "fix" our parent. When achieving this, even to a minor degree, we find a sense of peace among the phalanx of negative emotions which had overrun our countenance when we tried to force our opinions on to our aging parent.

Powerless is not helpless, and acceptance offers peace!

- **First, seek peace**

Some years ago, I remember being struck by a research report that appeared in the academic journal, *The Gerontologist.* The author explored the notion of rendering oneself purposefully helpless as it relates to the elder-caregiving situation. The researchers had studied and compared two groups of elder-caregivers: the first, Caucasians living in suburbs; the second, Native Americans living on reservations. In very creative ways, each group was asked to describe their caregiving roles and to express how they coped with the situation.

Differences between these two groups were striking. Whites reported a much greater need to control their caregiving role in general and their aging parent in particular. Over half of whites claimed that they either had control, or they were actively working to achieve control. Native Americans registered no such needs. Consequently, whites reported high levels of anger with themselves and their aging parents. Furthermore, whites registered levels of guilt commensurate with their higher levels of anger. Native Americans reported feeling neither anger nor guilt.

The coping strategies used by the two groups were decidedly different. Whites seemed to desire an ever-increasing want to "get on top of the situation," and to find solutions to problems presented by the caregiving situation. Native Americans were much more inclined to accept the aging condition and its consequences in ways that were noncontrolling. The study strongly implied that whites were inclined to resist the situation, while Native Americans "flowed" with it.

The attitudinal base expressed by whites seemed to be somewhat judgmental: "This shouldn't be the case; this should be different from what it is." Such a mentality created the breeding ground for the negative emotions of anger and guilt that whites experienced at higher levels. Native Americans, by contrast, acted from a very different attitudinal base. They followed what the researchers termed "passive forbearance." This approach to caregiving is one of creative acceptance. There seemed little if any resistance to reality, and very little judgment among them. Consequently, there emerged very little anger and guilt from their caregiving activities. Native Americans were happier and more at peace.

- **Seek to "let go" from the "get go," not as a last resort**

The *World Federation on Alcohol Abuse* has developed a fascinating definition of "letting go" which has clear application for the elder-caregiving situation. Try to determine how any of these sixteen descriptors of "letting go" might apply to your situation.

To let go:

 — does not mean to stop caring; it means I can't do it for someone else.

 — is not to cut myself off; it is the realization that I can't control another.

 — is not to enable, but to allow learning from natural consequences.

 — is to admit powerlessness, which means the outcome is not in my hands.

 — is not to try to change or blame another, but to make the most of myself.

 — is not to take care of, so much as to care for and to care about.

 — is not to "fix," but to be supportive.

 — is not to judge, but to allow another to be a human being—to be perfectly imperfect.

 — is not to be in the middle, arranging all the outcomes, but to allow others to affect their own destinies.

 — is not to be protective, but to permit another to face reality.

 — is not to deny, but to move toward acceptance.

 — is not to nag, scold, or argue, but to search out my own shortcomings and correct them.

 — is not to adjust everything to my desires, but to take each day as it comes and to cherish myself as God's child.

 — is not to criticize and regulate anybody, but to try to become what I dream I can be.

 — is not to regret the past, but to appreciate the present and grow and live for the future.

 — is to fear less and love more.

Naturally, not all of these will apply to your situation. Nonetheless, some certainly do. Take the ones that strike you, keep them in your mind, pray over them, and place them in your heart. Soon you will find that the burden you are carrying will be lighter; the sharp edge of anger that cuts you from time to time loses its fearsomeness; the angst and guilt that envelopes you loosens it grip. Gradually you will feel better; gradually, you will be moving toward creative acceptance.

Personal Sharing Questions

1. To what degree do you need to look at your caregiving relationship with "new eyes"?
2. To what degree do you feel that you have engaged in "creative acceptance" as described in this section? Describe.
3. Is your attitude about caregiving more "Caucasian" or "Native American," as they have been described in the section: "First, seek peace."
4. Of the sixteen descriptors of "letting go," choose three that you feel that you do quite well. Then go back and choose three that you feel you need to "work into" your caregiving.

THE NINTH FUNDAMENTAL
PRINCIPLE OF CAREGIVING:

&

Help Your Aging Parent Create an Autobiography

You may never have thought that one of the most fulfilling endeavors you and your aging parent can do together is create an autobiography of your parent's life. The task is not as daunting as it first sounds. This section outlines specific suggestions on how you can get started, and how to proceed with this vitalizing challenge. Creating an autobiography pays marvelous dividends for your aging parent, yourself, indeed the entire family. It is one of the most loving things that you can possibly do with your aging parent.

In the mid-seventies, an important book appeared: *Passages, Predicting Crises of Adult Life* by Gail Sheehy (E. P. Dutton & Company, Inc. 1976). Basically stated, Sheehy's ideas are that we continue to grow our entire lives, that we are constantly going through cycles of what she calls transitions and stages. Transitions last between one and three years. They are potentially chaotic periods between the end of one stage and the beginning of another. If there are any weak links in your life-chain, they are most likely to appear—and perhaps break—at the time of transition. If you are prone to depression, for example, it may appear first during a transition. The same would be the case for the onset of migraine headaches, ulcers, or whatever. The evidence suggests that all of this usually develops or worsens during the stressful time of a transition. So, transitional periods can be potentially traumatic, tempestuous, and extremely disconcerting. You are being pushed to make an important change.

Stages

Stages are those phases in your life that are linked together by transitions. Stages are typically seven to eight years in length (although this varies from person to person). In contrast to transitions, your life during these stages is basically placid. You are dealing with the same developmental tasks over and over. Your life is smooth. There is little change occurring, no crises to speak of, no bumps in the road, no critical junctures where you must decide which way you should go. Life during a stage sails along pretty well.

Transitions

Transitions are like bridges that connect stages. Some of the more prominent developmental transitions are: adolescence, followed by the launching phase where a person moves out of his or her home of origin. These are followed perhaps by "coupling," when you develop an intimate relationship with a special person. Then comes the so-called "age-thirty transition," when you deepen your resolve and develop commitments in your life. After that, comes the infamous mid-life transition, with all of its turmoil and decision-making. The family-launching transition is next, when the children leave home, followed by a time of reorganization called the "empty nest" transition. Preretirement is next; quickly on its heels comes the retirement event and the hopeful development of a new lifestyle.

It is important to think of transitions as challenges. Instead of backing into a transition with your eyes closed, welcome it as a time of challenge, an opportunity for growth, a time when you can change for the better. Research on stress has shown that the most potent stress reducer we have is our own attitude. Those who can conceive of stress as a challenge, as a time of commitment—as a chance to grow and change instead of withdrawing from it—are the most emotionally healthy.

When we apply this concept of transitions and stages to older persons, we come up with some very interesting notions. Some experts believe that the last decades of one's life are best defined as one long transition (rather than as a stage) because the older person is called upon to make so many changes during this period. This contradicts a commonly accepted belief that the later years are a time of serenity and calm when "the old couple" sit on the front porch in their rocking chairs and nothing much happens. Actually, a tremendous amount of change is taking place at this time. Think of the adjustments that older people are asked to make in their lives. Think of the coping mechanisms that have to be called upon. All this is happening at the same time that their resources are dwindling rather than growing.

Autobiography

Under the Second Fundamental Principle we covered the life arenas of career, family, faith, and leisure. Your aging parents perform roles in each of these life arenas, as do you, and they provide a rich treasure trove of material relating to relationships and bonding. You need to view your aging parents in these settings. Once you can do this, ask yourself: "How can I help my aging parent toward a more positive and meaningful attitude?" Here are a few things you can do.

- **Conduct a life review**

What does this mean? *Life Review* is a specialized term originated by Dr. Robert Butler. In every transition in your life, whether it is turning twenty-one, deciding on a mate, having children, experiencing "empty nest" syndrome, living through retirement backlash, etc., you conduct a kind of "life review" within yourself, perhaps without even realizing it. One of the hallmarks of a transition is that it is a time for looking back at your life and asking: "How am I doing? Is this the way I want to be conducting my life? Are there ways I could change it?" Normally, this natural process brings increased emotional health and allows individuals to "press on" in their developmental growth to the next stage.

Unfortunately, some people look back at their life and start digging up all sorts of regrets: "I should have done this. I should have done that. I wish I hadn't done this or that." Even though people know that such thinking is self-defeating, they still continue to engage in it. How does life review avoid this pitfall, this negative approach? Let's take a closer look at it.

Creating an autobiography is a life-giving process whereby your aging parent can review his or her life in a positive, orderly manner. This type of healthy reminiscing enables the person to search and uncover some of the deeper meanings underlying specific past events. Such soul-searching frequently helps your aging parent resolve any "unfinished business" or long-standing conflicts that may block him or her from fully capturing the joy and wisdom that can come from aging. That is why all people, especially older persons, like to talk about their life in earlier days. There is an instinctive desire to "tie up all the loose ends."

Of course, talking about the past all of the time is unhealthy, and may be a sign that a person needs professional help. This is called "selective memory," as when an older person obsessively grinds the proverbial axe over and over again. But well-ordered reminiscing, when done in a positive, sharing way, has been shown to help people, especially older ones, to live a richer, fuller, and healthier life. It is clear that this is not the idle wanderings of a deteriorating mind that can only "live in the past." Rather, it is the carrying out of a vital and enriching task of the present which brings wholeness and personal integrity.

Indications are that all older persons reminisce to a certain degree and that it is quite normal. They need to do this because their central life task in later years is to achieve integrity. They need to put their past life into a meaningful and purposeful whole. Creating an autobiography helps them achieve this vital goal of wholeness and completeness. Besides generating purpose, structured reminiscence aids in the rediscovery of past strengths, capabilities, and interests; fosters feelings and expressions of love; enhances the realization that aging is a time of continued personal growth; facilitates interactions; fights depression and demoralization; combats social isolation; and stimulates memory.

A Priest and His Father

Some years ago a priest came to me for counseling. He had been a priest for twenty-five years, and was then the pastor of a large parish. His mother had passed away, but his father was still living. It was with his father that the problem lay. His father evidently had been a very critical person; at least that's the way this priest remembered him. Every time we would talk, I'd hear how his dad had been so involved in his work, how they had moved from place to place, how he never saw much of him, and when he did there was always criticism. Finally I said:

> "Don't you think it is time to resolve this? You know we keep going round and round this bush and we are not addressing your central issue."
>
> "What do you mean, resolve this issue? My childhood is my childhood, what can I do? It is over. I can't relive it."
>
> "No, you can't. But you can resolve it, because this issue is having a tremendously negative impact upon your present life."

It was preventing him from breaking out, from gaining freedom and direction, and from getting to his next developmental stage. It had him locked in a transition. I said:

"You need to confront your father."

"Confront my father?" he exclaimed. "He's seventy-eight-years-old. It'll kill him."

"Well, he's lived seventy-eight years now. He's probably a pretty sturdy guy."

"No," said the priest, "this would do him in. I'm a priest, you know. I'm supposed to exemplify kindness and compassion and understanding and all those other wonderful attributes."

"You're hung up on your father. You are locked into a transition and can't get beyond it to begin your next developmental stage. You don't have any choice but to confront him."

Together we worked on how this priest could confront his father, how he could say: "Look, Dad, I have some heavy ideas that I've been carrying around since my childhood. I want to say these things to you because they're inside my heart and I need to vent them and I need you to listen. I don't need your condemnation or your criticism. I'm fifty-five years old. I'm trying to serve God. I think I'm doing what I'm supposed to be doing, and yet I've got this hang-up with you inside of me. Help me!"

That was a day of great tumult in the priest's life. Everything was turned upside down. He confronted his father. He resolved an issue. And do you know what happened? Not only did he come away with a whole new world-view, but his father—who had also been carrying around great guilt inside himself all these years—was able to get all his guilt out through this confrontation as well; so much so that within two months his father remarried. This seventy-eight-year-old man had also been stuck in a transition that he couldn't break out of, because of the push/pull antagonism that he felt from his son and the guilt that he was laying on himself. This resolution process brought the two of them together, and sparks flew all over the place. Those two men, father and son, walked away from that confrontation different people. They faced change;

they took action on a life transition. And both their lives got "unstuck" because of it.

Creating an Autobiography

This is but one example of the power of the autobiographical process. It can help people resolve deep-seated conflicts of the past, thereby aiding them in building quality relationships here and now. How is this done in practice? How do you go about conducting an autobiography with your aging loved one?

Recall what was emphasized earlier. Remember how everyone's life-experience can be viewed as played out in different *arenas*. Recall also that people go through *transitions* and *stages* as they live their lives. The central characteristic of these transitions and stages is that they are filled with much *emotion and feeling*. You can help your aging parent put his or her life into better and more healthy perspective, allowing it to become more understandable, clear, and meaningful for them, *if* you can bring together these three elements: 1) the life arenas, 2) the transitions, and 3) the stages. Putting these three together and combining them with the emotions experienced at those times, focusing them on your loved one's life story, constitute the essentials for creating a successful autobiography.

• **Enrich your visits with your aging parent**

It took me several years to finally notice the obvious: People generally have a difficult time visiting older people, especially if they are in a nursing home. This seemed especially true for adult children visiting their aging parents. They simply don't know what to say: "How's the food been, Mom? Been sleeping okay? How are your feet? Getting enough exercise?" To say the least, the quality of these visits leaves much to be desired. I was sure there was a better way. That's when the thought struck me: When you visit, why not spend thirty minutes working on an autobiography? Obviously, you can't go through a whole life in half an hour, but you have a lot to talk about and the autobiographical process actually never ends.

The interactions don't have to be stiff and formal:

- "How did you feel, Mom, when you had your first child?"
- "How about dating?"
- "How many dates did you have?"
- "What did Granddad say to you when you first started dating?"
- "How about school? What was it like in those days; do you remember some of your teachers' names in school?"
- "How did you feel at graduation?"

Your Parents' Emotional Life

Like most adult children, you may know very little about the *emotional* lives of your parents. You probably know most of the statistical and external "facts." You know they grew up through the Great Depression, which were tough times. They got married in 1939, had their first child in 1941, went through World War II with Dad in the service. You know all that sort of "stuff." But that's only an outer structure, sort of a facade of a person's life. That's not where people really *live*. Relationships are what give meaning to life; the very heartbeat of relationships are the emotions and feelings a person experiences as these life episodes are being lived.

Besides being very beneficial for your parents, your autobiography visits could also be very enriching for yourself. You needn't dread the next time you're going to see your mom. Rather, you can look forward to it, because while you're learning a new chapter of her life you'll also be discovering your own emotional roots. Try to get as much of it down in writing as you can, or record it on tape. After all, your parents will not be with you someday. There will be people three or four generations down the road who would very much enjoy hearing what this person, your parent, was actually like.

Perhaps some of you have already done this with your parents in some small way. Every person in this world has a story to tell, and each story is well worth hearing. If this is true of everyone, even of the strangers who pass you on the street, how much more valuable to have a record of significant happenings in your own parents' life, all told in their own words! Do you see the potential here? Instead of looking on those visits to your parents as drudgery, and thinking "What am I going to say today?" you can think about what you are going to do, and what you will learn once you arrive. The first few autobiographical visits might be awkward, with the note-taking or the microphone out there, but after a while it will all seem very natural. Incidentally, one of the nice things about making a recording is that you can leave the tape with your parent for him or her to replay during the week. Chances are, the listening will stir up other memories almost forgotten, precious memories about his/her early life, about happy and sad moments, about your grandparents or other relatives, about you, when you were very small.

Positive Effects

Once more, there are positive effects of the autobiographical process. First, it can help resolve conflict. There are times when everyone looks back and says: "I wish I'd done things differently then." It is at that point that you can look at your mom or dad and say: "You know, if I were in your shoes at that point in your life, I think I would have done the very same thing." "You would?" will be the response. "I think I would." Lo and behold, the conflict which had so tied up your parents begins to unravel. It is almost like receiving absolution. They are able to start thinking of themselves in more positive terms. They are more prepared to address the changes they need to make in their life now. They are free to create a greater peace, serenity, and wisdom in their hearts.

Let's say your mother begins to tell a story she has told many times before. What you should do is sit down with her and ask, "Mom, are you trying to tell me something? What is it in this story that's so important? What changed in your life because of it? Is this story, somehow, like what's going on in your life now?" If you can help your mother discover the underlying meaning of that story—why it is significant for her— you will be doing her a tremendous favor and showing her the highest honor. You have the power and the ability to do that. As a matter of fact, you are probably in a much better position to do that than a psychologist or anyone else.

Creating an autobiography is a very realistic attempt to put one's entire life in proper perspective. Have you seen your aging parents depressed at one time or another? Have you seen them anxious? You know how hopeless you feel when they are like that. What can you do? Now your answer can be that you will try to develop a quality relationship with them through autobiography.

How to Begin

Of course, this has to be done gently. You can't go home tonight, or to the nursing home, or wherever your parent is, and say: "Guess what we are going to do right now? We are going to take out this legal pad and we're going to create an autobiography." You might start with looking through an old photo album together. Or you might ask about the family tree, or relatives you've lost track of, or where certain mementos came from. Stories are always important.

There are so many questions to be asked. Think of all the changes that have occurred. Recall what was said in the Sixth Fundamental Principle about effective communication. People open up when they realize they are really being listened to. Respect your aging parents by using the full range of skills of active listening. Attend to them fully, both physically and psychologically; become a mirror to their thoughts and emotions by reflecting back what was said, by being concrete, by seeking clarification of events, relationships, and feelings.

Ask questions that begin with "what," "where," "how," or "when." Try not to ask "why" questions, because that calls for a rational response to situations or feelings which many times do not have a logical explanation. As much as possible, get to the feeling level. Try to follow up responses with questions like: "How did you feel when that happened?" "What was it like to be in that position?" In addition to our "thought memory," we also have a "feeling memory," which is all the emotion associated with a particular event, etc. Sharing feelings brings people even closer together.

Personal Sharing Questions

1. Do you think that you are currently in a stage or in a transition? Why? Describe.
2. Have you ever done any writing yourself?
3. Where are any records of the family, or genealogy, kept?
4. Does your aging parent like to tell stories? Does he or she reminisce a lot? Describe.
5. Do you remember your grandparents telling stories or reminiscing?
6. Do you think that having an autobiography of your aging parent would be looked upon favorably in your family? Describe.

The Tenth Fundamental Principle of Caregiving:

∽

Realize That You Are Never Alone in Your Caregiving—God Is Always There with You

It is through the elder-caregiving role that we learn to relate intimately with aging itself. When we take the time and interest to look deeply into the eyes of an elder, we encounter ourselves. We realize that the image we see in those eyes is our own: We too are aging. When we take the opportunity to look even deeper, we see a spark of life, a flash of the divine presence of God. Aging brings us into close contact with God in ways that we could not otherwise experience. The elder caregiving ministry is a privilege, a revered and exalted place of honor, where we catch glimpses of God. We come to realize that we are walking on holy ground, and that this moment is holy indeed!

- **Learn to open yourself to the special "caregiver's grace"**

I'm convinced that caregivers receive special grace from God! This grace is the power that God provides when God's children encounter a particularly difficult task. How many times have you looked back on a difficult time in your life and wondered, "How did I ever get through that?" It is God's grace. How is this special grace "packaged," how is it communicated? Our first step is to become open to it; we must believe that the special grace is there for us. We must believe that God does not ever abandon us or leave us devoid of the necessary tools, techniques, and help to achieve our task.

- **Recognize that your parent's aging, as well as your own, is part of the endless horizon of God's love**

How often have you lamented in puzzled frustration. "What is this process of aging all about? Why does God allow the losses, pain, and anguish associated with aging? Why would God give us the gifts of physical strength only to retract them as the years pass? When and how did the marvelous process of human maturation become the silent thief of aging?" Certainly, there must be a purpose. If aging is a part of God's plan, then what is there to gain from it?

Viewed through human eyes alone, aging is nothing more than a succession of losses ending in a painful descent into the oblivion of nothingness. Yet, as Christians, we are called to see beyond the frail barriers of human sight and view the endless horizon of God's love at work.

> *Aging challenges us to remember that God uses our natural human condition as a teaching aid for us to learn ever more personally the power of love.*

When viewed through the eyes of God, the process of aging becomes a vehicle for learning our true reality as children of God. We come to understand that there is no contradiction of God's promise of life in abundance. We simply learn to see life in an entirely different, spiritual light.

God wants the best for us. God gives us strength to do God's work here on this earth. However, God doesn't want us to lose sight of the fact that we are "in the world but not of the world" (see John 17:11-19). We are God's children and our journey is to God. As soon as we are born, we begin our march back toward God. As the losses of aging accumulate, we are called to understand that the persons we thought we were are not our true, completed selves.

For each year we live beyond early adulthood, small pieces of our physical strength, stamina, and sensitivity are taken away. This is not a cruel punishment, but rather a gentle reminder that we are headed toward a new life in the Spirit, toward a spiritual existence with God.

In her insightful book, *Necessary Losses* (Ballantine Books, 1986), Judith Viorst outlined her premise that human development—our transition from one life state to the next—is the product of our adaptation to life's losses rather than our accommodation to life's gains. She argues that in order for us to enter each new state of life, we must first leave (lose) the previous one. For example, we cannot grow into adulthood unless we first "lose" our childhood. Loss, then, becomes the driving force of maturation.

My experience as a professional counselor echoes this idea. It is loss—not gain—that produces growth. Therefore, the losses that aging brings in such rapid succession are not what they first appear to be. They are, instead, harbingers of a divine maturation that the world does not fully understand.

The growth brought about in aging is internal, and the world cannot see it. It can only be experienced. It is a growth in understanding, in peace, in wisdom. The plus side of aging— the gain in the loss—is spiritual.

• **Come to understand the spiritual gifts of caregiving**

The special spiritual gifts of caregiving can best be understood by viewing them through the lenses of virtues. Moral and spiritual character development over the life span is, in reality, the process of putting virtue into practice. Few experiences teach applied virtue better than caring for an aging parent. What classroom could teach patience better than caregiving? Where can we learn acceptance, peace, faith, harmony, trust, truth, gratitude, vision, inspiration, or humility better than when engaged in the caregiving process? Nowhere could we find a more productive curriculum in the virtues than in our caregiving efforts with our aging parents, relatives, and friends.

The losses we suffer through aging are gifts of grace, reminding us that we are headed for a greater reality. Our true essence is spiritual; our goal is the God who is Love. The physical losses of aging are not tragedies to be scorned, but signs leading us toward fulfillment in God.

As we grow into each new stage of life, we must leave behind the previous one; if we hang on to the last, we cannot move into the next. Aging is a process of growth—a progression of losses and gains strung in developmental succession—leading us to our glorious goal of being with God.

Aging is a vital, growth-filled, and even "youthfulness-producing" part of God's eternal plan for our salvation. We cannot shrink from it; we must embrace it with gusto!

The Primary Caregiving Virtues: Pathways to God

Beyond the caregiving virtue of acceptance, which was discussed in section eight, there are other virtues that give us a new vision of caregiving. We have open to us a reservoir of grace, wherein the energy that can propel us on our journey toward God resides. The "primary caregiving virtues" give us direction in our efforts at giving care from our very souls. They are like the keel on a sailboat, providing stability and security, and without which the sailboat could not go straight. Virtues plunge deep into the waters of our soul, tapping into the power of God that resides there.

- **Learn to see beyond the physical plane; learn to engage the primary caregiving virtues**
  There you will find God, there you will learn:

  Strength...when you can see how the elders you care for gain a fuller appreciation of life as a consequence of the physical maladies and annoyances of aging.

Trust...when you come to understand that the body is not the master of your soul.

Humility...when you see how some elders find personal triumph in the face of increasing dependency.

Hope...when you can smoothly give up yesterday's toys, tasks, and talents and replace them with today's reality.

Humor...when you can learn to laugh, as some of your elders do, in the face of grave loss.

Transcendence...when you can ascend the mountain of being inner-directed along with God, and move away from self-absorption.

Peace...when you can learn to gaze at a troubled world with serenity.

Empathy...when you can learn to find personal pleasure in the pleasures and good fortunes of others.

Love...when you can find delight in events not directly related to yourself.

Simplicity...when you can learn to invest in tomorrow's world while enjoying today's present.

Wholeness...when you can capture present-day, personal integrity from recognizing that God's hand has been on you all along!

All of these virtues come directly from God; they all emanate from the universal source of all power: Love. As we proceed in our caregiving, we gradually but persistently learn the power of love ever more deeply, as we successively learn the value of these virtues. In fact, caregiving is our classroom for learning God's ways, and for synthesizing all the various parts of ourself into a more authentic "whole." We are never alone in this quest; God's power is with us always. Our job is not to create the power, for we are powerless to do so; our job is simply to open ourselves up to the power which exists in abundance.

- **Foster spiritual development in your aging parent**

The arena of life where your aging parent can gain great personal satisfaction is the spiritual realm. This arena encompasses the relationship your aging parent shares with God. Some research studies have found that religious participation does not increase with age; actually, there appears to be a slight decrease. However, these studies were too narrowly constructed. They measured only participation in public religious activities, i.e., how often a person goes to church, as the sole criterion of religiousness. (Here a number of "external" factors, such as health and transportation problems, probably play large roles.) Moreover, it is very difficult to measure change in a person's internal relationship with God. My qualitative clinical observations of older persons tell me that, as maturation continues, elders normally do develop a more intimate relationship with God.

Adult children can foster spiritual development in their aging parents in many ways: praying with them, speaking about spiritual issues and relationships, joint Bible study, reading spiritual books and other materials aloud, listening to spiritually inspirational music, and by generally raising the level of awareness of and participation in religious activities and events. All of this effort will pay handsome dividends. Not only will your aging parent's faith development increase, but your relationship with her or him will take on a new dimension—a dimension that both of you can share with joy.

Personal Sharing Questions

1. Have you ever experienced the deep sense of spiritual presence that is outlined in the first paragraph of this section? Describe.

2. What do you think is God's purpose in giving us aging? Answer this question in as few words as possible.

3. Would you agree that our growth is dependent upon how well we transition through our losses? Discuss.

4. Which of the primary caregiving virtues do you rely upon in your caregiving? Explain.

5. Which of the primary caregiving virtues do you think need "shoring up"? Explain.

NEW PUBLICATION CATERS TO THE NEEDS OF SENIOR ADULT MINISTRY

Helping senior adults achieve spiritual and physical wellness throughout life has never been easier or more effective thanks to a new instructional resource from Liguori Publications, authored by Dr. Johnson.

Specifically crafted to the unique needs of those who work with senior adults, *Well, Wise & Whole* is a monthly training resource designed to build a greater understanding of senior adult ministry through effective, creative, faith-filled ideas for reaching seniors. Insightful, motivating, and inspirational, each monthly issue includes vibrant lessons and activities that can be used in both group and individual situations.

16 pages; 12 issues per year: $59.00
Available from Liguori Publications 1-800-325-9521.